# Improve Java Coding

## Best Practices for Effective Coding

IMPROVE
Java
CODING
*************************************************
Best Practices for Effective Coding
Real World Java Exercises
Including All of the Solutions
Sar Maroof

# Relevant Books By Sar Maroof

# Table of Contents

## What Does This Book Cover?

The journey of improving coding skills continues even after learning programming. The key question becomes: How can one write code professionally while addressing critical concerns such as code maintainability, code reusability, security issues, and memory leaks? This book focuses on real-world code examples, aiming to avoid unnecessary, boring, extended theoretical discussions. Instead, it goes straight to the point in coding and offers improvements with clear explanations.

Any building is eventually finished, but successful software is never truly finished. New features need to be built, causing the codebase to grow over time, and concerns about maintainability grow with it if programmers don't pay serious attention to it.

If you asked an expert and a junior programmer to write code for a specific program, you would realize that the expert accomplishes the goal with significantly less code than the junior programmer. Every extra line of code written unnecessarily creates more issues in terms of maintainability, opening the doors to hacking and security vulnerabilities.

The problem with coding is not that poorly written code doesn't work; the real problem is that it does. Therefore, it can be challenging for an inexperienced programmer to realize what a better version could be.

In this book, I will provide you with common mistakes through different pieces of code that function correctly, but I will also explain why it is crucial to avoid that kind of coding, even though it works.

Before diving into the chapters, let's highlight a few code issues to help you determine whether this book will benefit you. The code examples provide a preview of this book's approach to assist you in improving your Java coding. This book systematically addresses issues in the following steps:

- Presenting common code mistakes through a simple piece of code.
- Running the code to reveal unexpected outcomes.
- Explain the case and provide code improvements.

This approach ensures you understand how to manage similar code challenges in your programming work.

Sar Maroof

## About The Author

Sar Maroof is a professional software developer and database modeler, widely recognized as an accomplished author in these domains. With experience since the last twenties century, he has been involved in developing software for both large and small enterprises and has worked as a freelancer.
He is Sun-certified in Java Server Pages Technology (JSP )and Enterprise JavaBeans Programming (EJP). Additionally, Sar Maroof has experience providing instruction at the university level, teaching diverse groups of students. Furthermore, he has authored several books, including "Learn Java and Master Writing Code," "Improve Java Coding," and published programming books in other languages.

# Is This Book Right for You?

Here are some issues this book handles; if that is too difficult for you, I would recommend either starting with my other book for beginners, "Learn Java and Master Writing Code," or beginning with a relevant Java book before starting with this one.

## 1 Unsafe code

CH 7: Exercise 3

The following class Laptop declares the List of laptops as "private," which is fine. A private access modifier prevents other classes from directly changing the attributes' value. However, the class LaptopApp adds the brand "Acer" to the List and removes the "HP" " as shown in the output.

Improve the code to make it read-only so that other classes can only display the List but prevent them from updating it.

**Laptop.java**

```java
import java.util.ArrayList;
import java.util.List;

public class Laptop
{
  private List<String> laptops;
  {
    laptops = new ArrayList<>();
    laptops.add("Dell");
    laptops.add("IBM");
    laptops.add("HP");
    laptops.add("Lenovo");
  }
  public List<String> getListLaptops()
  {
    return laptops;
  }
}
```

**LaptopApp.java**

```java
public class LaptopApp
{
  public static void main(String[] args)
  {
    Laptop laptop = new Laptop();
    // adds the brand Acer to the list
```

```java
    laptop.getListLaptops().add("Acer");
    // removes the brand with index 2 which is HP
    laptop.getListLaptops().remove(2);
    System.out.print("\n"+laptop.getListLaptops());
  }
}
```

The output clearly shows that the brand Acer is added to the list, and HP is removed.

```
[Dell, IBM, Lenovo, Acer]
```

After improving the code, the list remains unchanged, as shown below.

```
The list is read-only.
[Dell, IBM, HP, Lenovo]
```

The solution(s) of this code issue and its explanation, including many more, are covered in this book.

## 2. Bank Issue

CH 7: Exercise 1

The following code consists of two classes: the BankAccount and the MainApp. The balance variable in the class BankAccount is not declared "private"; therefore, the customer can withdraw any amount of money regardless of his balance. If you declare the balance private, other classes cannot access the balance attribute. Improve the code so that other classes can only withdraw an amount lower than the balance.

Improve the code to check the following:

- A customer shouldn't be allowed to withdraw zero or a negative amount from his bank account.
- A customer shouldn't be allowed to withdraw an amount that exceeds his balance.
- For each transaction, the system should keep the date and time of the transaction.

## BankAccount.java

```java
public class BankAccount
{
  double balance = 3500.00;
}
```

## MainApp.java

```java
import java.util.Scanner;

public class MainApp
{
  public static void main(String[] args)
  {
    BankAccount bAccount = new BankAccount();
    System.out.printf("\nBalance is: $%.2f", bAccount.balance);
    Scanner scanner = new Scanner(System.in);

    System.out.print("\nEnter a positive amount: $");
    double amount = scanner.nextDouble();

    bAccount.balance -= amount;
    System.out.printf("Balance is: $%.2f ", bAccount.balance);
    scanner.close();
  }
}
```

The output shows that the customer withdraws $6000, and his balance becomes minus $-2500.

```
Balance is: $3500.00
Enter a positive amount: $6000
Balance is: $-2500.00
```

After improving the code, try to withdraw the following amounts to test the program: 6000, 0, -2000, and 2000, as shown below.

Output 1: The customer enters 6000, which exceeds his balance.

```
Balance is: $3500.00
Enter a positive amount: $6000

Insufficient balance

Balance is:         $3500.00
```

```
Transaction date: Fri Dec 22 14:00:26 CET 2023
```

Output 2: The customer enters an amount of zero.

```
Balance is: $3500.00
Enter a positive amount: $0

Transaction failed.

Balance is:          $3500.00
Transaction date: Fri Dec 22 14:01:11 CET 2023
```

Output 3: The customer enters a negative amount of -2000

```
Balance is: $3500.00
Enter a positive amount: $-2000

Transaction failed.

Balance is:          $3500.00
Transaction date: Fri Dec 22 14:01:52 CET 2023
```

Output 4: The customer enters an amount lower than his balance.

```
Balance is: $3500.00
Enter a positive amount: $2000

Balance is:          $1500.00
Transaction date: Fri Dec 22 14:02:25 CET 2023
```

The solution(s) of this code issue and its explanation, including many more, are covered in this book.

# 3. Initializer

CH 13: Quiz 1

In the following code, the "main" method body is empty. What happens if the code is compiled and run? What is your explanation for the output?

**Bird.java**

```java
public class Bird
{
  int age1 = getAge(2);
```

```
  Bird()
  {
     int age2 = getAge(4);
  }
  static
  {
     System.out.print(getAge(6));
  }

  static int age4 = getAge(8);
  int age5 = getAge(20);

  public static int getAge(int age)
  {
     System.out.print(age);
     return age;
  }
  public static void main(String[] args)
  {
  }
}
```

Select the correct answer.

a. This code writes "668" to the standard output.

b. This code writes "68" to the standard output.

c. This code writes "6" to the standard output.

d. This code writes "8" to the standard output.

e. This code writes "null" to the standard output.

f. This code writes nothing to the standard output.

The solution(s) of this code issue and its explanation, including many more, are covered in this book.

# 4. Efficient Coding

CH 5: Example 4b

In the following code, the method display creates three columns. Suppose you need one, two, three, four, and an unfixed number of columns. How do you apply that feature in the code? An option is to write a separate method for each number of columns; That option is time and code-consuming.

Improve the code to create tables with any number of columns you need by updating the following code with minimum changes.

**Table.java**

```java
public class Table
{
  final String SIGN = "*";
  final String SPACE = "   ";

  public void display(String title1, String title2, String title3)
  {
    String titleText = "";
    String underTitle = "";
    String newLine = "\n";

    titleText += title1 + SPACE;;
    underTitle += SIGN.repeat(title1.length()) + SPACE;

    titleText += title2 + SPACE;;
    underTitle += SIGN.repeat(title2.length()) + SPACE;

    titleText += title3 + SPACE;;
    underTitle += SIGN.repeat(title3.length()) + SPACE;

    System.out.print(titleText + SPACE + newLine);
    System.out.print(underTitle);
  }
  public static void main(String[] args)
  {
    Table tb = new Table();
    System.out.println("\n.... Three arguments ....\n");
    tb.display("Product", "Brand", "Price");
  }
}
```

Output:  Three arguments are passed through the method display

```
.... Three arguments ....

Product   Brand   Price
*******   *****   *****
```

The output after improvement of the code shows that one, two, three, four, five, or more columns can be created.

```
.... One Column ....

Product
*******
.... Two Columns ....

Product    Brand
*******    *****
.... Three Columns ....

Product    Brand    Price
*******    *****    *****
.... Four Columns ....

Product    Brand    Price    Category
*******    *****    *****    ********
.... Five Columns ....

Product    Brand    Price    Category    Type
*******    *****    *****    ********    ****
```

The solution(s) of this code issue and its explanation, including many more, are covered in this book.

# 5. Garbage Collection GC

CH 13: Quiz 3

Which is the earliest line in the MainApp class code, after which the object "computer" created on line 1 is eligible for garbage collection? Assuming no compile optimization is done. Prove the correctness of your answer if someone needs help understanding it.

**MainApp.java**

```java
public class MainApp
{
  private Computer computer;

  void setComputer(Computer computer)
  {
    this.computer = computer;
  }
  public static void main(String[] args)
  {
    Computer computer = new Computer(); //..1
```

```
    MainApp ma = new MainApp();   //.........2
    ma.setComputer(computer); //............3
    computer = new Computer(); //...........4
    computer = null; //.....................5
    ma = new MainApp(); //..................6
  }
}
```

**Computer.java**

```java
public class Computer
{
  String brand = "DELL";
}
```

Select the correct answer.

a. After line 1.

b. After line 2.

c. After line 3.

d. After line 4.

e. After line 5.

f. After line 6.

g. It is impossible to determine that.


The solution(s) of this code issue and its explanation, including many more, are covered in this book.

# 6. Overriding Methods

CH 9: Polymorphysm Quiz 2

The constructor of the superclass Person invokes the method printName, which is overridden in the subclass Freelancer.

What happens if you compile and run the code? Support your explanation with evidence.

**Person.java**

```java
public class Person
{
  String name = "Robert ";

  public Person()
```

```java
  {
    printName();
  }
  void printName()
  {
    System.out.print(name);
  }
}
```

**Freelancer.java**

```java
public class Freelancer extends Person
{
  String name = "Emma ";

  void printName()
  {
    System.out.print(name);
  }
  public static void main(String[] args)
  {
    Freelancer freelancer = new Freelancer();
  }
}
```

Select the correct answer.

a. This code writes "Robert" to the standard output.

b. This code writes "Emma" to the standard output.

c. This code writes "Emma Robert" to the standard output.

d. This code writes "Robert Emma" to the standard output.

e. This code writes nothing to the standard output.

e. This code writes "null" to the standard output.

The solution(s) of this code issue and its explanation, including many more, are covered in this book.

# 7. Avoid Magic Number

CH 14: Exercise 2

The following code allows the user to guess a secret number generated randomly by the program. It is unclear in the code how many times users are allowed to guess the number. Can you find that number and improve the code? To clarify to other programmers, how often can a user guess the secret number?

**Secret.java**

```java
import java.util.Scanner;

public class Secret
{
  public static void main(String[] args)
  {
    int rsn = 0; // rsn = random secret number
    int gsn = 0; // gsn = guess number

    int[] arraySecret = { 1, 2, 3, 4, 5, 6, 7, 8, 9, 10 };

    rsn = RandomElement.getRandom(arraySecret);
    /*
     * uncomment the following line to display
     * the generated secret number
     */
    // System.out.println("\nRandom secret number: " + rsn);
    Scanner input = new Scanner(System.in);
    System.out.print("\nEnter a guess number from 1 to 10: ");
    int i = 0;

    // Check if next input is int
    while (input.hasNextInt())
    {
      i++;
      gsn = input.nextInt();

      if(gsn == rsn)
      {
        System.out.println("Guess  " + gsn + " is correct.");
        break;
      }

      if(i >= 3)
      {
        System.out.println("Secret nr was: " + rsn);
        break;
      }
      System.out.print("Incorrect, please try again: ");
    }
    System.out.print("Application is closed");
    input.close();
  }
}
```

**RandomElement.java**

```java
import java.util.Random;

public class RandomElement
{
  int[] arraySecret = { 1, 2, 3, 4, 5, 6, 7, 8, 9, 10 };

  static int[] intArray = { 1, 2 };

  public static int getRandom(int[] array)
  {
    int rnd = new Random().nextInt(array.length);
    return array[rnd];
  }
}
```

Output

```
Enter a guess number from 1 to 10: 6
Incorrect, please try again: 5
Guess  5 is correct.
Application is closed
```

The solution(s) of this code issue and its explanation, including many more, are covered in this book.

# 8. Rusable Code

CH 14: Exercise 1

The client requests to display all the objects in the application, as shown below.

```
**************************
            Vehicle
**************************
Brand: .............. BMW
Color: .............. Brown
Fuel: .............. Gasoline
```

One of the essential coding principles is to be reusable, which is not applied in the following program.

Improve the code and make it reusable and accessible for all the other objects to be displayed, as shown in the output.

**Vehicle.java**

```java
public class Vehicle
{
  private String brand;
  private String color;
  private String fuel;

  public Vehicle(String brand, String color, String fuel)
  {
    this.brand = brand;
    this.color = color;
    this.fuel = fuel;
  }
  public void display()
  {
    System.out.println("****************************");
    System.out.println("           Vehicle          ");
    System.out.println("****************************");
    System.out.println("Brand: ............... " + brand);
    System.out.println("Color: ............... " + color);
    System.out.println("Fuel: ............... " + fuel);
  }
  public static void main(String[] args)
  {
    Vehicle vh = new Vehicle("BMW", "Brown", "Gasoline");
    vh.display();
  }
}
```

The solution(s) of this code issue and its explanation, including many more, are covered in this book.

## 9. Operator

CH 3: Quiz 5

What is the output of the following code? Clarify the answer.

**Product.java**

```java
public class Product
{
  static double price = 20;

  public static void main(String[] args)
  {
    if(price == price++)
    {
      price++;
```

```
      if(price == price++)
      {
        ++price;
      }
    }
    else
    {
      price += 8;
    }
    System.out.print(price);
  }
}
```

Select the correct answer.

a. This program writes "20.0" to the standard output.

b. This program writes "21.0" to the standard output.

c. This program writes "28.0" to the standard output.

d. This program writes "22.0" to the standard output.

e. This program writes "24.0" to the standard output.

The solution(s) of this code issue and its explanation, including many more, are covered in this book.

# 1. Classes, Objects, and Constructors

Java is an object-oriented programming language that allows one to build computer programs using objects that interact and communicate with each other. Each object contains variables(attributes) and methods which they work together. Java sees everything as an object, so people, animals, plants, and things around you are treated as objects.

Examples of objects are customers, companies, computers, tables, movies, mobiles, animals, students, plants, etc.

## Instantiating Objects From a Class

To start writing a program, you must create a class, a blueprint, or a template from which individual objects are created. Below is explained how to create a class. Once you create a class, you can instantiate unlimited objects from it.

## Class and Object Example

We use the following example to clarify how Java deals with classes. Suppose you are asked to write a small program for a company from which you can buy movies.

The company needs the following information about the films for now.
1. The title
2. The running time
3. The price

The mentioned data are called the attributes or the variables of the class. To write this simple program, we will take the following steps.

1. Creating a class
2. Instantiating objects from the class
3. Assigning values to the object's attributes
4. Accessing attribute's values
5. Displaying or printing attribute values

# Steps to Create the Movie App

## 1. Creating a Class

Each Java class is stored in a file with the name of the class and the extension ".java." In this case, we keep the class "Movie" in the file "Movie.java."

- A class starts with the Java keyword "class," followed by the name of the class and a block of code, as shown in the following example.
- The name of the classes starts with an uppercase.
- The company wants to store the title, running time, and the price of the movies.
- We declare variables for these three attributes.
- The names of attributes in Java start with lowercase letters.
- Each attribute starts with a data type or variable. We use the following three data types in this example, as shown in the table below.
- The main method to execute the Movie class should be defined, as shown in the code below.

## Table 1:  Data Types

| Data types | Used for |
| --- | --- |
| String | The string type is used in Java to combine symbols, numbers, and letters, such as names and texts. |
| int | The int type is used for integers such as ages and numbers without decimals. |
| double | The double type is used for decimal numbers such as prices and salaries. |

## *Example 1A: Creating a Class*

Below is a simple class movie created.

**Movie.java**

```java
// create a class
public class Movie
{
  // the attributes(variables)
  String title;
  int runnigTime; // minutes
  double price;
}
```

**MovieApp.java**

```java
public class MovieApp
{
  //the main method to execute the code
  public static void main(String[] args)
  {

  }
}
```

# 2. Instantiating Objects From a Class

- We can create as many movie objects as we need. For example, we make two objects for the movies "The Godfather" and "The Matrix".

- The name of an object starts with a small letter.

- Every object should have a name; you may choose any meaningful name for the objects you create.

- In the following example, we create the object movie1 for The Godfather and the object movie2 for The Matrix. The objects in our model contain the titles, the running time, and the prices of the movies.

- We can create an object by writing the class name and then the object's name. This is followed by the equal sign and the Java keyword "new." The class name ends with open and closed parentheses; further statements in Java end with a semicolon, as shown below.

> **Notice**
>
> Choosing the names is essential to organize your program.

## *Example 1B: Instantiating Objects*

We instantiate movie1 and movie2 objects from the class Movie.

**Movie.java**

```java
// create a class
public class Movie
{
  // the attributes(variables)
  String title;
  int runnigTime; // minutes
  double price;
}
```

**MovieApp.java**

```java
public class MovieApp
{
  //the main method to execute the code
  public static void main(String[] args)
  {
    // create object movie1
    Movie movie1 = new Movie();
    // create object movie2
    Movie movie2 = new Movie();
  }
}
```

# 3. Assigning Values to the Variables

To assign values to the variables, we use the object's name separated from the variable name by a dot (.), then the equal sign, and, at last, the variable's value.

The following statements assign the values "The Godfather, 177, 22.55" respectively to the variables title, running time, and price of the object movie1.

> **Notice**

The value of a string should be between quotes, as shown below.

Assigning values to the attributes title, running time, and price of the movie1 object.

## *Example 1C: Assigning Values to Attributes*

The below code shows how values are assigned to the attributes(variables) of the objects movie1 and movie2.

**Movie.java**

```java
// create a class
public class Movie
{
  // the attributes(variables)
  String title;
  int runnigTime; // minutes
  double price;
}
```

**MovieApp.java**

```java
public class MovieApp
{
  //the main method to execute the code
  public static void main(String[] args)
  {
    // create object movie1
    Movie movie1 = new Movie();
    /*
     * assign values to the
     * attributes of the object movie1
     */
    movie1.title = "The Godfather";
    movie1.runnigTime = 177;
    movie1.price = 22.55;
    // create object movie2
    Movie movie2 = new Movie();
    /*
     * assign values to the
     * variables of the object movie2
     */
    movie2.title = "The Matrix";
    movie2.runnigTime = 136;
    movie2.price = 24.65;
  }
}
```

Creating object movie2 and assigning values to its attributes follows the same process as the previous object movie1.

## 4. Displaying the Attribute Values

The previous code doesn't contain errors, but nothing will be displayed in the standard output if you compile and run it. The program only memorizes the titles, running times, and prices of two movie objects, The Godfather and The Matrix. That is comparable with human memory when you remember the multiplication tables. For example, you know that 6 x 5 equals 30, but you answer when someone asks you or you need it.
The program only displays or prints the values when the programmer decides when and where to show those values.

## 5. Accessing Attribute Values

To access the variables of the objects, you can use the name of the object and the variable name separated by a dot "." as shown below. In this step, we ask the program to write the objects "movie1 and movie2" data to the standard output. Everyone can memorize the data of the two movies of our example. Still, the program's power is that it can remember almost unlimited data of unlimited objects, which is beyond humans' capability. In the following examples, we ask the program to show the programmed data using the following statement.

```java
System.out.print(movie1.runnigTime + " minutes, ");
```

## *Example 1D: Movie Code*

By following the previous steps, we can write the following code.

**Movie.java**

```java
public class Movie
{
  // the attributes(variables)
  String title;
  int runnigTime; // minutes
  double price;
}
```

**MovieApp.java**

```java
public class MovieApp
{
  //the main method to execute the code
  public static void main(String[] args)
  {
    // create object movie1
    Movie movie1 = new Movie();
    /*
     *  assign values to the
     *  variables of the object movie1
     */
    movie1.title = "The Godfather";
    movie1.runnigTime = 177;
    movie1.price = 22.55;
    // create object movie2
    Movie movie2 = new Movie();
    /*
     *  assign values to the
     *  variables of the object movie2
     */
    movie2.title = "The Matrix";
    movie2.runnigTime = 136;
    movie2.price = 24.65;
    // print movie data;
    System.out.print(movie1.title + ", ");
    System.out.print(movie1.runnigTime + " minutes, ");
    System.out.println("$" + movie1.price);
    System.out.print(movie2.title + ", ");
    System.out.print(movie2.runnigTime + " minutes, ");
    System.out.println("$" + movie2.price);
  }
}
```

Below is the output of the code.

```
The Godfather, 177 minutes, $22.55
The Matrix, 136 minutes, $24.65
```

## Object References

The previous examples show how to create objects. The names of the
objects, movie1, and movie2, are references to two different objects.
It is possible to create one or more references to a single object. Below, we
make three references to the same object, namely movie1, movie2, and
movie3.

# *Example 2: Movie Code*

All three references, movie1, movie2, and movie3, refer to the same object, and the value of the variable title of all three objects is "The Godfather." If you compile and run the following code, the same title is written to the standard output for all three object references.

## MovieApp.java

```java
public class MovieApp
{
  //the main method to execute the code
  public static void main(String[] args)
  {
    // create object movie1
    Movie movie1 = new Movie();
    movie1.title = "The Godfather";
    /*
     * create references movie2 and movie3
     * to point to the same object
     */
    Movie movie2 = movie1;
    Movie movie3 = movie2;
    // print movie data;
    System.out.println("Movie1 title: " + movie1.title);
    System.out.println("Movie2 title: " + movie2.title);
    System.out.println("Movie3 title: " + movie3.title);
  }
}
```

Output

```
Movie1 title: The Godfather
Movie2 title: The Godfather
Movie3 title: The Godfather
```

-

## Notice

In the memory chapter, I will explain what happens in the stack and the heap memory when two references point to the same object.

# Constructors

A constructor is a particular method with the same name as the class name in which it exists. Constructors don't return values; unlike methods, you can use a constructor to instantiate objects and initialize their instance variables. Sometimes, creating more than one constructor in a class is practical. That will be covered later in this chapter.

## Constructors With Arguments

It is essential to understand that the default (no-argument) constructor can only be called if the class has no constructor. You can no longer invoke the default constructor when you define a constructor with one or more arguments. You can use a constructor with parameters to assign values to the instance variables. In the following class, Movie, three constructors are defined: the first one is a no-argument constructor, the second one is a constructor with two, and the third one is a constructor with three arguments. Therefore, you can no longer call the default constructor to instantiate objects if you remove the no-argument one in the following example.

## Why Use Multiple Constructors?

Using multiple constructors is very practical because we often need to display only some of the object's attributes and ignore the rest. Suppose that users search for only the title of a movie and its price. Why bother with all the attributes of the objects when they are unnecessary at that moment?

Sometimes, a class has many attributes, and we have only to assign the values of the attributes we see relevant to display.
Occasionally, we must have all the values of the object's attributes when creating it. That would hinder instantiating the object if we have only one constructor with all the attribute values needed to pass through. However, we can always assign the missing values of the attributes later to the object.

## Example 3: Movie Code

The following example demonstrates multiple movie constructors: the no-argument, the two-argument, and the three-argument constructor.

**Movie.java**

```java
public class Movie
{
  // the attributes(variables)
  String title;
  int runnigTime; // minutes
  double price;
  //no-argument constructor
  public Movie()
  {
    System.out.println("no-argument constructor");
  }
  //a constructor with two arguments
  public Movie(String title, int runnigTime)
  {
    this.title = title;
    this.runnigTime = runnigTime;
  }
  // a constructor with three arguments
  public Movie(String title, int runnigTime, double price)
  {
    //calling the two-argument constructor using "this"
    this(title, runnigTime);
    this.price = price;
  }
}
```

**MovieApp.java**

```java
public class MovieApp
{
  public static void main(String[] args)
  {
    // calling the no-argument constructor
    Movie movie1 = new Movie();
    Movie movie2 = new Movie("The Godfather", 177);
    Movie movie3 = new Movie("The Matrix", 136, 18.35);

    // print the attributes movie1
    System.out.println("--------movie 1----------");
    System.out.println("Title:          " + movie1.title);
    System.out.println("Running time: " + movie1.runnigTime);
    System.out.println("Price:          " + movie1.price);

    // print the attributes movie2
```

```java
        System.out.println("--------movie 2----------");
        System.out.println("Title:          " + movie2.title);
        System.out.println("Running time: " + movie2.runnigTime);
        System.out.println("Price:          " + movie2.price);

        // print the attributes movie3
        System.out.println("--------movie 3----------");
        System.out.println("Title:          " + movie3.title);
        System.out.println("Running time: " + movie3.runnigTime);
        System.out.println("Price:          " + movie3.price);
    }
}
```

Let's study the output of the previous code that creates three objects with the
constructors of no-arg, two-arg, and three-arguments of the class Movie.

Output

```
no-argument constructor
--------movie 1----------
Title:          null
Running time: 0
Price:          0.0
--------movie 2----------
Title:          The Godfather
Running time: 177
Price:          0.0
--------movie 3----------
Title:          The Matrix
Running time: 136
Price:          18.35
```

The first object is created by calling the "no-argument constructor." The text
"no-argument constructor" is printed because the constructor's body is
executed. We didn't assign any values to that object's attributes; therefore,
the values of the attributes are the standard values that Java determines. The
string is null, the int value is 0, and the standard double value is 0.0.

The second object calls the constructor with two arguments: the title and the
running time. Both values are assigned, but the price value isn't set.
Therefore, the price of the movie is given the standard double value, which
is 0.0.

You might have expected a code similar to the one below for the three-argument constructor. The following code works, too, but by programming, it is crucial to reuse your code instead of copying and pasting it. Using the keyword "this(title, running-time)," we call the two-argument constructor and reuse its code.

```java
public Movie(String title, int runnigTime, double price)
{
   this.title = title;
   this.runnigTime = runnigTime;
   this.price = price;
}
```

The code of the example

```java
// a constructor with three arguments
public Movie(String title, int runnigTime, double price)
{
   //calling the two-argument constructor
   this(title, runnigTime);
   this.price = price;
}
```

## Overloading Constructors

A class can have multiple constructors, which is what we mean by overloading constructors. By overloading, the constructors should have different numbers or types of parameters (arguments).
Applying object-oriented programming concepts focuses on redundancy and reusing your code.

## Calling a Constructor Within a Constructor

In the above example, we can reuse the code of the two-argument constructor within the three-argument constructor by calling it with "this" keyword. As follows:

```java
this(title, runnigTime);
```

## Quiz 1: Employee Constructor

What happens when the following program is compiled and run?

**Employee.java**

```java
public class Employee
{
  String name = "Ronald";
  int age;

  Employee()
  {
    this.name = "Jack";
  }
  Employee(String name)
  {
    this();
  }
  Employee(String name, int age)
  {
    this("David");
  }
  public static void main(String[] args)
  {
    Employee emp = new Employee("John", 22);
    System.out.println(emp.name);
  }
}
```

Select the correct answer.

a. This code writes "John" to the standard output.

b. This code writes "David" to the standard output.

c. This code writes "Jack" to the standard output.

d. This code writes "Ronaldo" to the standard output.

e. This code writes "null" to the standard output.

f. This code writes nothing to the standard output.

## Quiz 2: Aircraft Constructor

What happens when the following program is compiled and run?

**Aircraft.java**

```java
public class Aircraft
{
```

```java
String brand;
int nrSeats;

Aircraft()
{
  this.nrSeats = 250;
  this.brand = "Airbus";
}
Aircraft(String brand)
{
  this();
  brand = "Hawker";
  nrSeats = 300;
}
public static void main(String[] args)
{
  Aircraft ac = new Aircraft("Boeing");
  System.out.println(ac.brand + ", " + ac.nrSeats);
}
}
```

Select the correct answer.

a. This code writes "Boeing, 250" to the standard output.

b. This code writes "Boeing, 300" to the standard output.

c. This code writes "Hawker, 300" to the standard output.

d. This code writes "Airbus, 300" to the standard output.

e. This code writes "null, 250" to the standard output.

f. The code causes an error.

## Quiz 3: Student Object Reference

What happens when the following program is compiled and run?

**Student.java**

```java
public class Student
{
  String name;

  public Student()
  {
    this.name = "Marco ";
    System.out.print("Robert ");
  }
  public Student(String name)
  {
```

```java
        this.name = name;
    }
    public static void main(String[] args)
    {
        Student st1 = new Student("Emma ");
        Student st2 = new Student("Anna ");
        Student st3 = new Student();
        st1 = st2;
        st3 = st1;
        st3 = null;
        System.out.print(st1.name);
    }
}
```

Select the correct answer.

a. This code writes "Emma" to the standard output.

b. This code writes "Anna" to the standard output.

c. This code writes "Robert, Anna" to the standard output.

d. This code writes "Marco" to the standard output.

e. This code writes "null" to the standard output.

f. The code causes an error.

## Exercise 1: Box Constructor

A company processes orders and sends the products in boxes to its customers. The sizes and shapes of the boxes are different. Some of the packages are cubes, and others are rectangular. The unique number of each Box is the same as the order ID and is known already.

Create a class "Box" with all the constructors that make your program convenient. By creating any objects of Box, a message should appear that "the box number is created."

Suppose the following program is written to convert the company's requirements to automate the process. As is shown below, you can create any boxes of any size using the following code.

Is there any way to improve the class Box?

**Box.java**

```java
public class Box
{
```

```java
  int boxNr;
  double width, height, depth;

  Box(int boxNr)
  {
    this.boxNr = boxNr;
    System.out.println("Box number " + boxNr + " is created!");
  }
  // calculate the volume
  double getVolume()
  {
    return width * height * depth;
  }
}
```

**BoxApp.java**

```java
public class BoxApp
{
  public static void main(String[] args)
  {
    Box box = new Box(100);
    box.width = 20;
    box.height = 10;
    box.depth = 2;
    System.out.println("Volume:  " + box.getVolume());
  }
}
```

Output

```
Box number 100 is created!
Volume:   400.0
```

## *Exercise 2: Customer Account*

Customers who register on a website should provide their first name and last
names. Customers who want to create an account should also provide their
email addresses, but that is only required by creating an account. Customers
who don't want to create an account can enter the letter "q" to quit, as shown
in the output below.

**Notice**

The scanner class in Java allows user input. User input is covered in the
following chapters of this book.

Improve the code of the customer and the MainApp classes. Define all the necessary constructors for the classes customer and account.

**Account.java**

```java
public class Account
{
    String email;
}
```

**Customer.java**

```java
public class Customer
{
  String firstname;
  String lastname;
  Account account;
}
```

**MainApp.java**

```java
import java.util.Scanner;

public class MainApp
{
  public static void main(String[] args)
  {
    /*
     *   the code below allows user input
     */
    Scanner input = new Scanner(System.in);

    System.out.print("Enter your firstname: ");
    String firstname = input.nextLine();

    System.out.print("Enter your lastname: ");
    String lastname = input.nextLine();

    System.out.print("Enter your email or q to quit: ");
    String email = input.nextLine();
  }
}
```

In the following output, the customer doesn't create an account but enters the letter "q" to quit.

```
Enter your firstname: Emma
Enter your lastname: Davids
Enter your email or q to quit: q

.... Your info ....
Firstname:      Emma
Lastname:       Davids
```

The following customer wants to create an account.

```
Enter your firstname: David
Enter your lastname: Smith
Enter your email or q to quit: david@mail.com

.... Your account ....
Firstname:      David
Lastname:       Smith
Email:          david@mail.com
```

Improve the given code so the program functions as in the previous output.

## Answers to the Quizzes and the Exercises

## Answer Quiz 1

- In the body of the main method, the employee object emp is instantiated, which calls the constructor Employee with two arguments.

- The constructor's body with a two-argument calls the constructor with a one-argument.

- The body of the constructor with one argument is called the no-argument constructor.

- In the body of the no-argument constructor, the value "Jack" is assigned to the name attribute.

- So, the statement System.out.println(emp.name) prints the name Jack to the standard output.

The correct answer is c.

## Answer Quiz 2

- In the body of the main method, the Aircraft constructor with one argument is called the Aircraft no-argument constructor this().
- The no-argument constructor assigns the value 250 to the attribute nrSeats. It also assigns the value of Airbus to the brand attribute.
- After calling the no-argument constructor, the following statement in the body of the one-argument constructor assigns the value Hawker to the brand and 300 to the nrSeats.
- The statement "this" is missing; therefore, the program uses the brand argument instead of the attribute.
- The value brand Airbus wouldn't be replaced with Hawker, but the value 300 of the nrSeats would replace the first value 250.

The correct answer is d.

```
Airbus, 300
```

By adding "this" to the brand, the program assigns the value of Hawker to the brand attribute, as shown below.

```
Aircraft(String brand)
{
  this();
  this.brand = "Hawker";
  nrSeats = 300;
}
```

Output

```
Hawker, 300
```

## Answer Quiz 3

- In the body of the main method, the objects st1, st2, and st3 are created.
- The no-argument constructor is called by creating the object st3, which prints the name Robert to the standard output.
- The st3 object later points to the st1 object and null, but it isn't used to print anything to the standard output.

- The statement within the main method prints the name of the student st1 to the standard output.

- The statement st1 = st2 points the reference st1 to the st2 object. By creating st2, the name Anna is passed through the constructor. So, the name Anna is printed to the standard output.

- The correct answer is c.

Output

```
Robert Anna
```

# Answer Exercise 1

The previous solution wasn't complete because it only allowed the creation of box objects by passing the box number. From the assignment, we understand that in many cases, the dimensions (width, height, depth) are known. In some instances, cubes with three equal dimensions or sides are used. We must add two more constructors to the class to make the program more flexible. We also need to reuse the constructor with the box number parameter.

**Box.java**

```java
public class Box
{
  int boxNr;
  double width, height, depth;
  Box(int boxNr)
  {
    this.boxNr = boxNr;
    System.out.println("\nBox number " + boxNr + " is created!");
  }
  Box(double length, int boxNr)
  {
    this(boxNr);
    width = length;
    height = length;
    depth = length;
  }
  Box(double width, double height, double depth, int boxNr)
  {
    this(boxNr);
    this.width = width;
```

```java
      this.height = height;
      this.depth = depth;
   }
   // calculate the volume
   double getVolume()
   {
      return width * height * depth;
   }
}
```

**BoxApp.java**

```java
public class BoxApp
{
   public static void main(String[] args)
   {
      Box box = new Box(100);
      Box box2 = new Box(5, 101);
      System.out.println("Volume: " + box2.getVolume());

      Box box3 = new Box(5, 7, 10, 102);
      System.out.println("Volume: " + box3.getVolume());
   }
}
```

Below is the output of the program.

```
Box number 100 is created!

Box number 101 is created!
Volume: 125.0

Box number 102 is created!
Volume: 350.0
```

## Answer Exercise 2

We add a one-argument constructor for the class Account and pass the email attribute to it.

For the customer class, it is practical to have two constructors; the first is for customers who want to register. Therefore, it only has arguments for the first and last names. The second constructor is used for customers who wish to register. Thus, the email is also passed as an argument through it.

**Account.java**

```java
public class Account
{
  String email;

  Account(String email)
  {
    this.email = email;
  }
}
```

## Customer.java

```java
public class Customer
{
  String firstname;
  String lastname;
  Account account;

  Customer(String firstname, String lastname)
  {
    this.firstname = firstname;
    this.lastname = lastname;
  }
  Customer(String firstname, String lastname, String email)
  {
    this(firstname, lastname);
    this.account = new Account(email);
  }
}
```

## MainApp.java

```java
import java.util.Scanner;

public class MainApp
{
  public static void main(String[] args)
  {
    Scanner input = new Scanner(System.in);
    System.out.print("Enter your firstname: ");
    String firstname = input.nextLine();
    System.out.print("Enter your lastname: ");
    String lastname = input.nextLine();
    System.out.print("Enter your email or q to quit: ");
    String email = input.nextLine();
    Customer customer;

    if(!email.equals("q"))
    {
      System.out.println("\n.... Your account ....");
      customer = new Customer(firstname, lastname, email);
    }
```

```java
    else
    {
      System.out.println("\n.... Your info ....");
      customer = new Customer(firstname, lastname);
    }
    System.out.println("Firstname:      " + customer.firstname);
    System.out.println("Lastname:       " + customer.lastname);

    if(customer.account != null)
    {
      System.out.println("Email:          " + customer.account.email);
    }
  }
}
```

# 2. User Input in Java

The concept of input and output is well known in programming. The input is
the data unknown by the program, while the output is the result of the
program's conclusion based on the input.

Suppose a website allows subscribers to register based on their ages and
annual income. A program can only decide whether a user is accepted or
rejected if the program receives the user's data.

Once the user enters the required information, the program processes the
information and makes a decision based on that. The information that the
user enters is known as input, while the conclusion that the program comes
with is called the program's output.

In this book, two Java input classes are covered, namely, the classes Scanner
and BufferedReader.

## Java Scanner Input Types

The scanner is a class in the Java util package used for acquiring the input of
primitive data types like int, boolean, double, and objects like strings. Using
the Scanner class in Java allows reading a user input in a Java program.
Scanner class allows a programmer to take the standard input stream in
Java. Several methods are offered to extract data from the stream.

> **Notice**
>
> I only use the class Scanner for simple examples and exercises in this
> chapter. However, it is essential to understand how input and output work
> because the following chapters will cover more complicated examples and
> exercises about input and output.

## Table 1: Methods of the Class Scanner

| Method | Description |
| --- | --- |
| nextBoolean() | Used for reading Boolean value |
| nextByte() | Used for reading Byte value |
| nextDouble() | Used for reading Double value |
| nextFloat() | Used for reading Float value |
| nextInt() | Used for reading Int value |
| nextLine() | Used for reading Line value |
| next() | `next()` can read the input only till the space. It can't read two words separated by a space. Also, `next()` places the cursor in the same line after reading the input. |
| nextLong() | Used for reading Long value |
| nextShort() | Used for reading Short value |

## *Example 1: User Input Using Scanner*

The following code demonstrates using the Scanner class to take user input.

**Register.java**

```java
import java.util.Scanner;

public class Register
{
  public static void main(String[] args)
  {
    System.out.println("------Input------");
    Scanner input = new Scanner(System.in);

    System.out.print("Enter your name: ");
    String name = input.nextLine();

    System.out.print("Enter your age: ");
    int age = input.nextInt();

    System.out.print("Enter your gender: ");
    char gender = input.next().charAt(0);

    System.out.print("Enter your wage: $");
```

```java
        double wage = input.nextDouble();
        String formattedString = String.format("%.02f", wage);

        System.out.print("Are you married? true/false: ");
        boolean isMarried = input.nextBoolean();

        System.out.println("------Output------");
        // print the data
        System.out.println("Name:       " + name);
        System.out.println("Age:        " + age);
        System.out.println("Gender:     " + gender);
        System.out.println("Wage:      $" + formattedString);
        System.out.println("Married:    " + isMarried);
        input.close();
    }
}
```

Output of the code

```
------Input------
Enter your name: Emma Smith
Enter your age: 24
Enter your gender: Female
Enter your wage: $3500
Are you married? true/false: false

------Output------
Name:       Emma Smith
Age:        24
Gender:     F
Wage:       $3500.00
Married:    false
```

# User Input the Class BufferedReader

The BufferedReader is another class in Java used to take user input by reading text from a character-input stream. It provides a convenient way to read arrays and text.

## *Example 2: User Input BufferedReader*

The following code demonstrates using the BufferedReader class to take user input.

**Register.java**

```java
import java.io.BufferedReader;
import java.io.IOException;
import java.io.InputStreamReader;

public class Register
{
  // Main Method
  public static void main(String[] args) throws IOException
  {
    // Creating BufferedReader Object
    BufferedReader input = new BufferedReader
                            (new InputStreamReader(System.in));
    // String reading internally
    System.out.print("Enter your name: ");
    String name = input.readLine();

    // Integer reading internally
    System.out.print("Enter your age: ");
    int age = Integer.parseInt(input.readLine());

    // Printing String
    System.out.println("Your name is: " + name);
    // Printing Integer
    System.out.println("Your age is: " + age);
  }
}
```

Output

```
Enter your name: David
Enter your age: 32

Your name is: David
Your age is: 32
```

## *Exercise 1: Convert Centimeters to Inches*

Write a program that allows users to enter a length in centimeters; the program converts the length into inches. Use the following formula to calculate the length in inches.

1cm = 0.3937 inches.

## Input

Before starting to write code, determine what the input is. Which data does the program need from the user?

## Output

The output calculates the length that the user enters in Inches.

Once the user's input is known, the program uses the formula that converts the length from cm to inches.

In the following output, the user enters the length of 10 cm. The program uses the formula to calculate it in inches.

Output of the program

```
.... Input ....
Enter a length in cm: 10

.... Output ....
10.0 cm = 3.937 Inches
```

## *Exercise 2: The Sum of Two Numbers*

Write a program that allows users to enter two numbers; the program calculates the sum of the numbers.

## Input

The unknown part is the two numbers that the user should provide, and that is the input.

## Output

We use the two numbers for the output and calculate the sum for the user. In the following output, the user enters the numbers 465 and 500. The program calculates the output.

```
.... Input ....
Enter the first number: 465
Enter the second number: 500

.... Output ....
465 + 500 = 965
```

## *Exercise 3: Fahrenheit to Celsius*

Write a program that converts any temperature in Fahrenheit entered by users to a Celsius degree.

## Input

The input is to ask the user to enter the degree in Fahrenheit.

## Output

Based on the user input, we need the following formula to calculate the Fahrenheit degree.

Tc is the Celsius degree that we need for the calculation.

Tf is the Fahrenheit degree entered by the user.

**Tc = (Tf - 32) × 5/9.**

Below is the program output for the value 32 Fahrenheit entered by the user.

```
.... Input ....
Enter a degree in Fahrenheit: 32

.... Output ....
32.0 Fahrenheit = 0.0 Celsius
```

## Answers to the Quizzes and the Exercises

## Answer Exercise 1

We create the class LengthConverter. This class allows user input. Therefore, we import the class Scanner from the Java util package. The result can only be calculated if the user input is available.

The first step is to ask the user to enter the length in cm. The input in this example is assigned to the **lCm** (length in cm) variable.

**LengthConverter.java**

```java
import java.util.Scanner;

public class LengthConverter
{
  public static void main(String[] args)
  {
    Scanner input = new Scanner(System.in);
```

```java
        System.out.println("\n.... Input ....");

        System.out.print("Enter a length in cm: ");
        double lCm = input.nextDouble();

        double lInch = lCm * 0.3937;
        System.out.println("\n.... Output ....");
        System.out.println(lCm + " cm"+ " = "+lInch+" Inches");
    }
}
```

Output

```
.... Input ....
Enter a length in cm: 10

.... Output ....
10.0 cm = 3.937 Inches
```

# Answer Exercise 2

In this example, importing the Scanner class is necessary to allow user input. Two variables of type int are declared, and respectively, the values that the users enter are assigned to them.

The program displays the sum calculation and displays it as shown in the code.

**Sum.java**

```java
import java.util.Scanner;

public class Sum
{
  public static void main(String[] args)
  {
    Scanner input = new Scanner(System.in);

    System.out.println("\n.... Input ....");
    System.out.print("Enter the first number: ");
    int nr1 = input.nextInt();

    System.out.print("Enter the second number: ");
    int nr2 = input.nextInt();
    int sum = nr1 + nr2;

    System.out.println("\n.... Output ....");
    System.out.println(nr1 + " + " + nr2 + " = " + sum);
  }
}
```

Output

```
.... Input ....
Enter the first number: 465
Enter the second number: 500

.... Output ....
465 + 500 = 965
```

# Answer Exercise 3

We ask the user to enter the degree in Fahrenheit. The output is the calculation using the formula given by the exercise.

**TempConverter.java**

```java
import java.util.Scanner;

public class TempConverter
{
  public static void main(String[] args)
  {
    Scanner input = new Scanner(System.in);

    System.out.println("\n.... Input ....");
    System.out.print("Enter a degree in Fahrenheit: ");
    double tf  = input.nextDouble();
    double tc = (tf - 32) * 5/9;

    System.out.println("\n.... Output ....");
    System.out.println(tf + "Fahrenheit = " +tc+ " Celsius");
  }
}
```

Output

```
.... Input ....
Enter a degree in Fahrenheit: 32

.... Output ....
32.0 Fahrenheit = 0.0 Celsius
```

# 3. Java Language Quick Guide

This quick guide explains the basic programming concepts, such as operators, conditional statements, and loops.

## Data Types and Variables

Java provides certain data types and guarantees a standard initial value of those types, as shown below!

### Table 1: Variable's Default Values

| Type | Default value |
| --- | --- |
| boolean | False |
| byte | 0 |
| short | 0 |
| int | 0 |
| long | 0L |
| char | u0000 |
| float | 0.0f |
| double | 0.0d |
| object reference | Null |

## Operators

Java provides different types of operators to manipulate variables, as shown below.

### Table 2: Arithmetic Operators

Arithmetic operators are used to work with numbers and mathematical expressions.

| Arithmetic operators | Description |
| --- | --- |

| | |
|---|---|
| + (Addition) | 3 + 6 returns 9 |
| - (subtraction) | 8 – 6 returns 2 |
| * (Multiplication) | 4 * 5 returns 20 |
| / (Division) | 20/4 returns 5 |
| % (Modulus) | Divides left operand by right operand and returns remainder<br>17 % 5 returns 2, because<br>17/5 = 3 and the rest is 17 – (5 * 3) = 2 |

## Table 3: Relational Operators

Relational operators are used to evaluate two operands for equality. The answer is either true or false.

| Relational Operators | Description |
|---|---|
| == Equal | Checks the value of two operands. If they are equal returns true else returns false.<br>int x = 5, int y = 6;<br>(x == y) returns false. |
| != Not equal | Checks the value of two operands. If they are not equal returns true else returns false.<br>int x = 5, int y = 6;<br>(x != y) returns true. |
| > Greater than | If the left operand value greater than the right one returns true else returns false.<br>(8 > 5) returns true. |
| < Less than | If the left operand value is smaller than the right one returns true else returns false.<br>(8 < 5) returns false. |
| >= Greater or equal | If the left operand value is greater or equal to the right one, returns true else returns false.<br>(7 >= 7) returns true. |
| <= Less than or equal | If the left operand value is smaller or equal to the right one returns true else returns false.<br>(6 <= 9) returns true |

# Table 4: Conditional (Logical) Operators

Conditional statements use conditional operators. The conditional statement
types that Java supports are AND (&&) and OR (||)

| Conditional operators | Description |
| --- | --- |
| && AND | && combines two boolean variables and returns true only if both of its operands are true.<br>if (3 > 2 && 4 < 6 ) returns true<br>if(6 > 3 && 3 < 2) returns false |
| \|\| OR | \|\| combines two boolean variables and returns true if one or both of its operands are true.<br>If(1 > 2 \|\| 6 < 13) returns true |
| ?: | Ternary operator<br>Shorthand formulas<br>if-then-else statement<br>int n = 6;<br>int p = (n == 6) ? 4 : 5;<br>The above statement means the following.<br><br>if(n == 6) {<br>  p = 4;<br>} else {<br>  p = 5;<br>}<br>Returns 4, because n is equal to 6. |

# Table 5: Assignment Operators

An assignment operator is used to assign values to a variable. The variable
is usually at the left side of the equation, and the right side of the operand is
a value that is assigned to the variable.

| Assignment operators | Description |
| --- | --- |
| = Assignment | Assigns values to variables.<br>x = a-b assigns the value of a-b to x |
| += Addition | x += 5 is equivalent to x = x + 5 |

| | |
|---|---|
| -=Subtraction | x -= 4 is equivalent to x = x – 4 |
| *= Multiplication | x *= 3 is equivalent to x = x * 3 |
| /= Division | x /= 2 is equivalent to x = x/2 |
| %= Modulus | x %= 2 is equivalent to x = x % 2<br>example 1<br>int x = 21;<br>x % 4; is equivalent to x = x % 4<br>= 21 % 4 = 1.<br>x = 21 % 4 = the rest of 21 divided by 4 = 1.<br>example 2<br>int x = 17;<br>x % 3; means x = de rest van 17/3 = 2. |

## Table 6: Unary Operators

A unary operator is usually used to increment or decrement the values of a variable. For incrementing a variable's value by one, we typically use ++, and -- is used to decrement the value of a variable by one.

| Unary operators | Description |
|---|---|
| ++ Increment | Increments a value by 1.<br>int x = 20;<br>++ x returns 21 |
| - - Decrement | Decrements a value by 1<br>int x = 20;<br>- - x returns 19 |
| ! | ! reverses the value of a boolean expression.<br>boolean isDefected = false;<br>! isDefected returns true. |

## Table 7: Type Comparison Operator

| Comparison operator | Description |
|---|---|
| instanceof | Compares an object to a specified type. |

Objects are later explained in this book.

# Conditional Statements

## If... Statements

The if statement tells the program to execute a particular code block only if the condition is true.

## If... Else Statements

The if statement allows executing a particular code block only if the condition is evaluated as true. If the condition returns false, the else block is executed.

By working with a chain of if statements, the program checks all the conditions of the if blocks. When the if block's condition returns true, the block is executed; otherwise, the block is ignored.

> **Notice**
>
> If the chain of the if conditions ends with an else statement, the else block is only executed if the condition of the last if block returns false.

## If... Else if Statements

By working with a chain of if/ else-if statements, the program starts with the first if statement. If the condition is evaluated as true, the block associated with that statement is executed. The program ignores the remaining part of the chain. If the condition returns false, the block is ignored, and the program continues with the following else-if statement. As soon as the condition of a particular block returns true, the block is executed, and the rest of the program is ignored.

> **Notice**
>
> If the chain of the else-if conditions ends with an else statement, the else block is only executed if the conditions of all the other blocks are false.

## Switch ... Case Statements

The switch statement is used to choose from several options. In such cases, if-else statements are impractical because you need to write a lot of code to achieve the same goal that can be easier achieved with a switch statement.

## *Quiz 1: Discount Calculation*

A company offers product discounts based on the customer's age and a special discount for students. In this company, a combination of two or more discounts is possible.

What happens when the following program is compiled and run?

**Item.java**

```java
public class Item
{
  public static void main(String[] args)
  {
    int age = 18;
    boolean isStudent = true;
    double price = 100;
    double discount = 0;

    // block 1
    if(age <= 20)
    {
      discount = price * 0.20;
    }

    // block 2
    if(isStudent)
    {
      discount += (price * 0.50);
    }
    // block 3
    else
    {
      discount += (price * 0.10);
    }
    price -= discount;
```

```java
      System.out.printf("\nPrice is:$%.2f", price);
   }
}
```

Select the correct answer.

a. The code writes Price is $100.00.

b. The code writes Price is $30.00.

c. The code writes Price is $80.00.

d. The code writes Price is $70.00.

e. The code writes Price is $90.00.

## Quiz 2: Discount Calculation

Let's change the variable values in the previous example and notice the differences.

What happens when the following program is compiled and run?

**Item.java**

```java
public class Item
{
   public static void main(String[] args)
   {
      int age = 17;
      boolean isStudent = false;
      double price = 100;
      double discount = 0;

      // block 1
      if(age <= 20)
      {
         discount = price * 0.20;
      }

      // block 2
      if(isStudent)
      {
         discount += (price * 0.50);
      }
      // block 3
      else
      {
         discount += (price * 0.10);
      }
```

```java
    price -= discount;
    System.out.printf("Price is:$%.2f", price);
  }
}
```

Select the correct answer.

a. The code writes Price is: $100.00.

b. The code writes Price is: $ 30.00.

c. The code writes Price is: $80.00.

d. The code writes Price is: $70.00.

e. The code writes Price is: $90.00.

## Quiz 3: Salary Based on Programming Level

A company offers a base salary of $1,500 for their applicants.
- If the applicant is a junior programmer, he receives a $2,000 extra salary above the base salary.
- The applicant gets $ 4,000 above the base salary if he is an Intermediate programmer.
- The applicant receives $ 6,000 extra above the base salary if he is a senior programmer.

The following code is written based on the above information.
What is the output of the following program?

**Programmer.java**

```java
public class Programmer
{
  public static void main(String[] args)
  {
    char level = 'J'; // J(Junior), M(Intermediate), S(Senior)
    double salary = 1500;

    // block 1
    if(level == 'J')
    {
      salary += 2000;
    }
    // block 2
    else if(level == 'M')
```

```java
    {
      salary += 4000;
    }
    // block 3
    else if(level == 'S')
    {
      salary += 6000;
    }
    // block 4
    else
    {
      salary += 300;
    }
    System.out.printf("Salary is: %.2f", salary);
  }
}
```

Select the correct answer.

a. The code writes Salary is: $1800.00.

b. The code writes Salary is: $3500.00.

c. The code writes Salary is: $5500.00.

d. The code writes Salary is: $7500.00.

e. The code writes Salary is: $1500.00.

## *Quiz 4: Salary Based on Programming Level*

Let's change the variable values and rerun the program. This time, we tested the program for a senior programmer.

What is the output of the following code?

**Programmer.java**

```java
public class Programmer
{
  public static void main(String[] args)
  {
    char level = 'S'; // J(Junior), M(Intermediate), S(Senior)
    double salary = 1500;

    // block 1
    if(level == 'J')
    {
      salary += 2000;
    }
```

```java
      // block 2
      else if(level == 'M')
      {
         salary += 4000;
      }
      // block 3
      else if(level == 'S')
      {
         salary += 6000;
      }
      // block 4
      else
      {
         salary += 300;
      }
      System.out.printf("Salary is: %.2f", salary);
   }
}
```

Select the correct answer.

a. The code writes Salary is: $1800.00.

b. The code writes Salary is: $3500.00.

c. The code writes Salary is: $5500.00.

d. The code writes Salary is: $7500.00.

e. The code writes Salary is: $1500.00.

## *Quiz 5: Unary Operators*

Understanding the unary operators ++ & --

What happens when the following program is compiled and run?

**Product.java**

```java
public class Product
{
   static double price = 20;

   public static void main(String[] args)
   {
      if(price == price++)
      {
         price++;

         if(price == price++)
         {
```

```
            ++price;
        }
    }
    else
    {
      price += 8;
    }
    System.out.print(price);
  }
}
```

Select the correct answer.

a. This program writes "20.0" to the standard output.

b. This program writes "21.0" to the standard output.

c. This program writes "28.0" to the standard output.

d. This program writes "22.0" to the standard output.

e. This program writes "24.0" to the standard output.

## Quiz 6: Student Grades

What is the output of the following program?

**Student.java**

```java
public class Student
{
   public static void main(String[] args)
   {
      int grade = 8;
      String gradeText = "";
      switch (grade)
      {
         case 0: case 1: case 2: case 3: case 4: case 5:
            gradeText = "Insufficient";
            break;
         case 6: case 7:
            gradeText = "Sufficient";
            break;
         case 8: case 9:
            gradeText = "Good";
         case 10:
            gradeText = "Excellent";
            break;
         default:
            gradeText = "Invalid";
```

```
    }
    System.out.println(gradeText);
  }
}
```

Select the correct answer.

a. This program writes "Sufficient" to the standard output.

b. This program writes "Insufficient" to the standard output.

c. This program writes "Good" to the standard output.

d. This program writes " Good Excellent" to the standard output.

e. This program writes "Excellent" to the standard output.

f. This program writes "Invalid" to the standard output.

# Iteration (Loop) Statements

Iteration or loop statements are used to handle processes that are repeated more than once. There are three types of loops in Java, namely, for, while, and do while.

A loop consists of two parts:

1. A control part: the repetitions are determined in the control part.

2. A body: the body contains the statements that have to be repeated.

## For Loop

The for-loop is used very frequently in Java. The for-loop is a good choice if you know how often a loop must be repeated.

## While Loop

The while loop begins with an evaluation of a condition. If the condition returns true, the body will be executed. The execution of the loop's body is repeated as long as the condition returns true. If the condition returns false, the loop will be terminated.

# Do-While Loop

The body of the do-while loop is executed at least once because the condition is evaluated after executing the body. The execution of the loop is continued until the condition returns false. When the condition is false, the loop is terminated.

## *Quiz 7: For-Loop Oil Class*

What is the output of the following program?

**Oil.java**

```java
public class Oil
{
  public static void main(String[] args)
  {
    double price = 40;

    for (int year = 1; year <= 5; year++)
    {
      price += 3;
    }
    System.out.printf("Price is: %.2f", price);
  }
}
```

Select the correct answer.

a. The output of the code is Price is: 55.00.

b. The output of the code is Price is: 43.00.

c. The output of the code is Price is: 46.00.

d. The output of the code is Price is: 49.00.

e. The output of the code is Price is: 52.00.

f. The output of the code is Price is: 40.00.

The following while loop repeats the execution, starting with the number's initial value of 0 till the number becomes 3. Each time, the number ++ increases the number by one.

## *Example 1: While Loop*

What is the output of the following code?

**WhileLoop.java**

```java
public class WhileLoop
{
  public static void main(String[] args)
  {
    int number = 0;
    System.out.println();

    while (number < 4)
    {
      number++;
      System.out.println("Number is: " + number);
    }
  }
}
```

- The number has an initial value of zero. The head of the while-loop checks whether the number is smaller than 4.

- If the number is smaller than four, the loop's body is executed, and the statement number ++ increments its value by 1.

- Once the number value reaches four, the loop's control returns false because four is not smaller than 4. Therefore, the loop is terminated, as shown in the output.

Output

```
Number is: 1
Number is: 2
Number is: 3
Number is: 4
```

## *Example 2: Do-While Loop*

What is the output of the following program?

**DoWhileLoop.java**

```java
public class DoWhileLoop
{
  public static void main(String args[])
  {
    int number = 1;
    do
```

```java
  {
    number++;
    System.out.print("\nNumber is : " + number);
  }
  while (number < 3);
}
}
```

- The initial value of the variable number is one.
- The do-block is always executed the first time.
- The statement number ++ increments the value of the number by one.
- The control of the loop checks whether the value of the number is smaller than 3. If it is, the loop is executed; otherwise, it is terminated, as shown in the output.

Output

```
Number is : 2
Number is : 3
```

## Example 3: Basic For-Loop

What is the output of the following program?

**ForLoop.java**

```java
public class ForLoop
{
  public static void main(String[] args)
  {
    // basic for loop
    for (int i = 0; i < 5; i++)
    {
      System.out.println("i: " + i);
    }
  }
}
```

- The head of the for loop starts with an initial value of the variable i, zero.

- Each time, the loop's head increments the value of the variable i by one.
- The loop's body is executed as long as the variable i is smaller than five. Otherwise, the loop is terminated.

Output

```
i: 0
i: 1
i: 2
i: 3
i: 4
```

## Example 4: Basic Infinite For-Loop

What is the output of the following program?

**ForLoopInfinite.java**

```java
public class ForLoopInfinite
{
  public static void main(String[] args)
  {
    // infinite for loop
    for (;;)
    {
      System.out.println("Hi...");
    }
  }
}
```

There is no condition in the for loop (;;); therefore, the loop is infinite and has no limit.

Output: This infinite loop looks like a while(true) loop.

```
i...
Hi...
Hi...
Hi...
Hi...
Hi...
Hi...
```

## Exercise 1: Sum of Entered Numbers

Write a program that allows users to enter a number repeatedly. The program adds all the user-entered numbers and keeps the total sum. Once the sum of all the numbers equals or exceeds 100, the program is terminated, and the sum is displayed on the standard output. See the possible outputs.

Output 1: The user enters the numbers 3, 44, and 57. The program is terminated and displays the sum, which is 104.

```
Enter number 1: 3
Enter number 2: 44
Enter number 3: 57
Sum = 104
```

Output 2: The user enters the numbers 21, 30, 40, 4, 3, 2. The program is terminated and displays the sum, which is 100.

```
Enter number 1: 21
Enter number 2: 30
Enter number 3: 40
Enter number 4: 4
Enter number 5: 3
Enter number 6: 2
Sum = 100
```

## Exercise 2: Display Triangle

Write a program that asks users to enter a symbol. The program creates and displays a triangle of the entered symbol.
In the first output, the user enters an asterisk symbol.

```
Enter a Symbol: *
*
**
***
****
*****
```

```
******
*******
********
```

In the second output, the user enters an at symbol.

```
Enter a Symbol: @
@
@@
@@@
@@@@
@@@@@
@@@@@@
@@@@@@@
@@@@@@@@
```

## Answers to the Quizzes and the Exercises

## Answer Quiz 1

The code contains a chain of if statements.

- The program executes each block of a chain of if statements individually. So, block one is executed because the customer is 18 years old and is younger than 20 years and receives a discount of %20.

- The program checks further block 2, and it is executed because the customer is a student. The customer receives an extra discount of 50 percent.

- Block 2 is the last if-block that returns true because the customer is a student.

- Block 3 or the else block is only executed if the last if-block, block 2, returns false. In this case, the customer is a student. Therefore, block two is executed, but block three is ignored.

The correct answer is b.

Output

```
Price is:$30.00
```

## Answer Quiz 2

The code contains a chain of if statements.

- The program executes each block of a chain of if-statements individually. So, block 1 is executed because the customer is 17 years old and is younger than 20 years.

- The program checks further block 2, which is ignored because the customer is not a student.

- Block 2 is the last if-block. Therefore, block 3 or the else-block is executed because the customer is not a student.

The correct answer is d.

## Answer Quiz 3

A company offers a base salary of $1,500 for their applicants.

- By a chain of if else-if statements, only one condition is true. So, the programmer cannot simultaneously be a junior, Intermediate, and a senior programmer.

- The first block code checks whether the programmer is a junior programmer, which is true.

- Based on that, his total salary would be the base salary + 2000.

- Total salary = 1500 + 2000 = 3500$

The correct answer is b.

## Answer Quiz 4

The same as the previous example, but this time, block 3 is executed; therefore, the salary is:

- Total salary = 1500 + 6000 = 7500$

The correct answer is d.

## Answer Quiz 5

- The statement if(price == price++) returns true because the price value is incremented by one after the evaluation.
- The statement price ++ increments the value of the price by another one. So, the price is now 22.
- The following statement if(price == price++) returns true, and the price will be incremented by one after the evaluation. By now the price is 23.
- The statement ++price increments the value of the price by one again.
- The if statement returns true; therefore, the else statement is ignored, and the last price value becomes 24.

The correct answer is e.

## Answer Quiz 6

- The grade 8 doesn't match the first seven cases but fits case 8.
- The expected grade text is "Good". However, the program searches further for the following case because there is no break statement under case 8.
- So, the code prints Excellent to the standard output and breaks.
- The correct answer is e.

## Answer Quiz 7

- Due to inflation, the price of oil increases yearly by $3.
- The for statement indicates that when the variable year equals one, execute the loop's body.
- After each execution, the statement year ++ increases the year's value by 1.
- The process is repeated till the value of the year becomes 5.
- By each execution of the loop block, the statement price += 3 increases the price by 3.
- So, the initial price value is 40, which is increased 5 times by 3.

The correct answer is a.

# Answer Exercise 1

It is easier to use a while loop because it is unknown how many times the user enters a number. When the number reaches or exceeds 100, the program is terminated.

**MaxSum.java**

```java
import java.util.Scanner;

public class MaxSum
{
  public static void main(String[] args)
  {
    Scanner input = new Scanner(System.in);
    int sum = 0;
    int i = 0;

    while (true)
    {
      i++;
      System.out.print("Enter number " + i + ": ");
      int nr = input.nextInt();
      sum += nr;

      if(sum >= 100)
      {
        break;
      }
    }
    System.out.println("Sum = " + sum);
    input.close();
  }
}
```

# Answer Exercise 2

In this program, we know how many times the loop is executed. Therefore, we use the for loop.

**Triangle.java**

```java
import java.util.Scanner;

public class Triangle
{
  public static void main(String[] args)
```

```java
{
  Scanner input = new Scanner(System.in);

  System.out.print("\nEnter a Symbol: ");
  String sign = input.nextLine();
  String line = "";

  for (int i = 0; i < 8; i++)
  {
    line += sign;
    System.out.print(line + "\n");
  }
  input.close();
}
}
```

# 4. Arrays and Java Collections

## Arrays

An array is a collection of elements of the same type. The number of the elements of arrays is fixed, and each element has a position in the array. The position of the elements is indicated by an integer value called index, which starts from 0. The number of elements that can fit in an array is called length. An array in Java is not a primitive data type but an object.
You can define an array as follows:

1. Declare a name for the array.
2. You can create an array object as usual with the keyword new.
3. Specify the data type of the array.
4. Specify the length of the array.
5. Add elements to the array.

See the following example:
Here, below, we define an array of integer-type data. The size of the array is 7, which indicates that only seven elements can fit in it.

```
int [] myArray = new int [7];
```

## The Class ArrayList

An ArrayList is a data structure that allows you to collect elements in a list. An ArrayList is often used because its size can change. It is one of the classes in the Java library that contains different methods to add, remove, and sort elements in alphabetical order and more. Each element of an ArrayList has an index that starts from 0. To use an ArrayList in your classes, import it from the Java library as shown below. ArrayList implements the List interface.

```
import java.util.ArrayList;
```

The table below shows some methods of ArrayList for more details see ArrayList in the Java standard API documentation.

## Table 1: ArrayList Methods

| Method | Return data type | Description |
| --- | --- | --- |
| add(int index, E element) | void | Inserts an element at a specified position in the list. |
| add(E element) | boolean | Appends the specified element to the end of the list. |
| get(int index) | Element | Returns the element at a specified position. |
| remove(int index) | Element | Removes the element at the specified position |
| size() | int | Returns the number of elements in the list. |

# Maps in Java

A map is an object that stores pairs of elements in the form of keys and values. A key is a unique element that can be used to find the corresponding value.

# The Map Interface

A map is an interface that replaces the abstract class Dictionary. It combines pairs of data known as keys and values. Keys in a map must be unique; therefore, duplicate keys are not allowed. Each key is associated with a single value.

# The HashMap class

The HashMap class is similar to the HashTable class but is not synchronized and allows null values. If you require the collection elements to maintain a specific order, it is advisable not to choose HashMap. Because it provides no guarantees regarding the map's order, it does not ensure that the order will remain constant over time. HashMap implements the interface Map.

## Table 2: HashMap Methods

| Method | Return data type | Description |
|---|---|---|
| put(key, value) | V | Inserts a key-value pair into the HashMap. |
| get(key) | V | Retrieves the value associated with the specified key |
| remove(key) | V | Removes the key-value pair associated with the specified key |
| containsKey(key) | boolean | Checks if the HashMap contains a specific key |
| size() | int | Returns the number of key-value pairs in the HashMap |

## *Quiz 1: Array of Strings*

What is the output of the following program?

**Brand.java**

```java
public class Brand
{
  public static void main(String[] args)
  {
    String[] brands = new String[3];
    brands[1] = "Dell";
    brands[2] = "HP";
    brands[0] = "IBM";
```

```java
    for (int i = 0; i < brands.length; i++)
    {
      System.out.print(brands[i] + " ");
    }
  }
}
```

Select the correct answer.

a. The output of the code is IBM Dell HP.

b. The output of the code is Dell HP IBM,.

c. The output of the code is HP Dell IBM.

d. The output of the code is IBM, Dell.

e. The output of the code is IBM.

## Quiz 2: ArrayList Object

What is the output of the following program?

**Employee.java**

```java
import java.util.ArrayList;
import java.util.List;

public class Employee
{
  List<String> employees = new ArrayList<String>();

  Employee()
  {
    this.employees = new ArrayList<String>();
    employees.add("Emma ");
  }
  Employee(List<String> employees)
  {
    this.employees = employees;
    this.employees.add("Jack ");
  }
  public static void main(String[] args)
  {
    Employee emp1 = new Employee(); //................line 1
    emp1.employees.add("David "); //..................line 2
    Employee emp2 = new Employee(emp1.employees); //..line 3

    for (String emp : emp2.employees) //..............line 4
    {
```

```java
        System.out.print(emp);
    }
  }
}
```

Select the correct answer.

a. The output of the code is Jack.

b. The output of the code is Jack David .

c. The output of the code is Emma Jack.

d. The output of the code is Jack David Emma.

e. The output of the code is Emma David Jack.

f. The output of the code is nothing.

## Quiz 3: ArrayList Object

What is the output of the following program?
This quiz is the same as the previous one, but we changed the reference
emp2 to emp1 on line 4 this time.

**Employee.java**

```java
import java.util.ArrayList;
import java.util.List;

public class Employee
{
  List<String> employees = new ArrayList<String>();

  Employee()
  {
    this.employees = new ArrayList<String>();
    employees.add("Emma ");
  }
  Employee(List<String> employees)
  {
    this.employees = employees;
    this.employees.add("Jack ");
  }
  public static void main(String[] args)
  {
    Employee emp1 = new Employee(); //................line 1
    emp1.employees.add("David "); //.................line 2
```

```
    Employee emp2 = new Employee(emp1.employees); //..line 3

    for (String emp : emp1.employees) //..............line 4
    {
       System.out.print(emp);
    }
  }
}
```

Select the correct answer.

a. The output of the code is Jack.

b. The output of the code is Jack David .

c. The output of the code is Emma Jack.

d. The output of the code is Jack David Emma.

e. The output of the code is Emma David Jack.

f. The output of the code is nothing.

# Ways to Iterate Over a List in Java

## Basic for Loop

### *Example 1: Basic for Loop*

What is the output of the following program?

**Country.java**

```
public class Country
{
  String name;
  String capital;

  public Country(String name, String capital)
  {
    this.name = name;
    this.capital = capital;
  }
}
```

**MainApp.java**

```java
import java.util.ArrayList;

public class MainApp
{
  public static void main(String[] args)
  {
    Country country1 = new Country("France", "Paris");
    Country country2 = new Country("United States", "Washington");
    Country country3 = new Country("Russia", "Moscow");

    ArrayList<Country> countries = new ArrayList<Country>();
    countries.add(country1);
    countries.add(country2);
    countries.add(country3);
    System.out.println();

    // basic for loop
    for (int i = 0; i < countries.size(); i++)
    {
      System.out.println(countries.get(i).name + ", "
                         + countries.get(i).capital);
    }
  }
}
```

- In the previous example, we created a country ArrayList and added three countries.
- We printed each country's name and capital within the for loop block.

Output

```
France, Paris
United States, Washington
Russia, Moscow
```

# Enhanced for Loop

The enhanced for loop simplifies the way to iterate through collections. This feature is introduced in Java version 5.

We apply enhanced for loop in the following example.

## *Example 2: Enhanced for Loop*

The output of this code is the same as in the previous example. We only used enhanced for loop.

**MainApp.java**

```java
import java.util.ArrayList;

public class MainApp
{
  public static void main(String[] args)
  {
    Country country1 = new Country("France", "Paris");
    Country country2 = new Country("United States", "Washington");
    Country country3 = new Country("Russia", "Moscow");

    ArrayList<Country> countries = new ArrayList<Country>();
    countries.add(country1);
    countries.add(country2);
    countries.add(country3);
    // enhanced for loop
    for (Country country : countries)
    {
      System.out.println(country.name + " " + country.capital);
    }
  }
}
```

Output

```
France, Paris
United States, Washington
Russia, Moscow
```

## Using Iterator

We can also use Iterators in Java to retrieve elements one by one. The following example shows how the Iterator works.

## *Example 3: Iterator Loop*

The output of the code is the same as in the previous examples. This code is only to demonstrate Iterator in Java.

**MainApp.java**

```java
import java.util.ArrayList;
import java.util.Iterator;

public class MainApp
{
  public static void main(String[] args)
  {
    Country country1 = new Country("France", "Paris");
    Country country2 = new Country("United States", "Washington");
    Country country3 = new Country("Russia", "Moscow");

    ArrayList<Country> countries = new ArrayList<Country>();
    countries.add(country1);
    countries.add(country2);
    countries.add(country3);
    // using Iterator
    Iterator<Country> iterator = countries.iterator();

    while (iterator.hasNext())
    {
      Country country = iterator.next();
      System.out.println(country.name + " " + country.capital);
    }
  }
}
```

Output

```
France, Paris
United States, Washington
Russia, Moscow
```

# For Loop Lambda Expression

The lambda expression is a block code through which you can pass a
parameter, which returns the result, as shown in the example below.

## *Example 4: Lambda for Loop*

The output of this code is the same as in the previous examples.

**MainApp.java**

```java
import java.util.ArrayList;
```

```java
public class MainApp
{
  public static void main(String[] args)
  {
    Country country1 = new Country("France", "Paris");
    Country country2 = new Country("United States", "Washington");
    Country country3 = new Country("Russia", "Moscow");

    ArrayList<Country> countries = new ArrayList<Country>();
    countries.add(country1);
    countries.add(country2);
    countries.add(country3);
    // for loop using lambda expression
    countries.forEach(country ->
    {
      System.out.println(country.name + " " + country.capital);
    });
  }
}
```

Output

```
France, Paris
United States, Washington
Russia, Moscow
```

# Method Reference

Method references are a way to increase Java code readability and allow to refer to methods or constructors without invoking them. There are several types of method references.

- Static method references
- Instance method references
- Constructor references

## *Example 5: Static Method References*

**Country.java**

```java
import java.util.Arrays;
import java.util.List;
```

```java
public class Country
{
  public static void main(String[] args)
  {
    List<String> countries = Arrays.asList("US", "DE", "IN");

    System.out.println("\n... Lambda expression...");
    countries.forEach(name -> System.out.println(name));

    System.out.println("... Static method reference...");
    countries.forEach(System.out::println);
  }
}
```

Output

```
... Lambda expression...
US
DE
IN
... Static method reference...
US
DE
IN
```

## *Example 6: Instance Method References*

### Display.java

```java
public class Display
{
  void print(String message)
  {
    System.out.println(message);
  }
}
```

### Country.java

```java
import java.util.Arrays;
import java.util.List;

public class Country
{
  public static void main(String[] args)
  {
```

```java
    List<String> countries = Arrays.asList("UK", "RU", "FR");

    System.out.println("\n... Lambda expression...");
    countries.forEach(message -> new Display().print(message));

    System.out.println("... Instance method reference...");
    Display display = new Display();
    countries.forEach(display::print);
  }
}
```

## Output

```
... Lambda expression...
US
DE
IN
... Static method reference...
US
DE
IN
```

# *Example 7: Constructor References*

### ConstructorInterface.java

```java
public interface ConstructorInterface
{
 // functional single abstract method interface
 Country create(String name);
}
```

### Country.java

```java
public class Country
{
  private String name;
  // one-argument constructor
  public Country(String name)
  {
    this.name = name;
  }
  public String getName()
  {
    return name;
  }
}
```

**MainApp.java**

```java
public class MainApp
{
  public static void main(String[] args)
  {
    // constructor reference with a functional interface
    ConstructorInterface constructorRef = Country::new;
    /*
     *  Creating an instance of a Country class
     *  with a constructor reference
     */
    Country instance = constructorRef.create("Constructor Ref");
    // Displaying the value from the created instance
    System.out.println("\nName: " + instance.getName());
  }
}
```

Output

```
Name: Constructor Ref
```

## *Example 8: Using HashMap*

The following code shows how to use a HashMap in Java.

**LanguageMap.java**

```java
import java.util.HashMap;
import java.util.Map;

public class LanguageMap
{
  static Map<String, String> languageMap =
                      new HashMap<String, String>();
  public static void addDataDisplay()
  {
    languageMap.put("en", "English");
    languageMap.put("fr", "French");
    languageMap.put("de", "German");
  }
  public static void getDataDisplay()
  {
    addDataDisplay();
    System.out.println();
    for (Map.Entry<String, String> entry : languageMap.entrySet())
    {
      String key = entry.getKey();
```

```java
        String value = entry.getValue();
        System.out.println(key + "   " + value);
      }
    }
  public static void main(String[] args)
  {
    getDataDisplay();
  }
}
```

Output

```
de  German
en  English
fr  French
```

## Exercise 1: Creating an English Dictionary

Add your code to the following program to create a dictionary that allows users to type an English word. The program prints a synonym of the word entered by the user, as shown in the output.

**EnDictionary.java**

```java
import java.util.HashMap;
import java.util.Map;
import java.util.Scanner;

public class EnDictionary
{
  Map<String, String> words = new HashMap<String, String>();
  public void addWords()
  {
    words.put("Go", "Walk");
    words.put("Buy", "Purchase");
    words.put("Happy", "Pleased");
    words.put("Translate", "Interpret");
    words.put("End", "Finish");
  }
  public static void main(String[] args)
  {
    EnDictionary enDict = new EnDictionary();
    enDict.addWords();
    Scanner input = new Scanner(System.in);
    System.out.print("\nEnter a word: ");
    // add your code here
  }
}
```

For output 1, the user enters "Go." The program prints the synonymous of the entered word in the dictionary.

```
Enter a word: Go
Synonymous is: Walk
```

For output 2, the user enters "End." The program prints the synonymous of the entered word in the dictionary.

```
Enter a word: End
Synonymous is: Finish
```

For output 3, the user enters "Great." The program prints that the word is not found.

```
Enter a word: Great
The word Great is not found!
```

## Exercise 2: Add Dishes to the Menu

Write a program enabling a restaurant manager to check whether a particular dish is on the menu. The program searches for it, and if it is found, the program mentions that. If the dish is not on the menu, the program adds it. When the program is run, the first line that appears is the current menu. If you run the program, the following are the possible outputs.

For output 1, the manager enters Fish, which is already on the menu.

```
Current Menu: [Rice, Pizza, Fish, Soup, Beef]
Add a dish to the menu: Fish
Fish is already on the menu.
```

For output 2, the manager entered Hamburger, which needs to be added to the menu.

```
Current Menu: [Rice, Pizza, Fish, Soup, Beef]
Add a dish to the menu: Hamburger
Hamburger is added: [Rice, Pizza, Fish, Soup, Beef,
Hamburger]
```

## Answers to the Quizzes and the Exercises

# Answer Quiz 1

- Three brands have been added to the array of brands.
- In the first position, index 0, the IBM brand is added to the array.
- The second position with the index 1 is Dell.
- The third brand with index 2 is HP.
- So, the output is IBM Dell, HP

The correct answer is a.

# Answer Quiz 2

- By creating the emp1 object on line 1, the name Emma is added to emp1's employees ArrayList.
- The name David is also added to its employees ArrayList on line 2
- When the object emp2 is created on line 3, the ArrayList employees of the emp1 object is passed to it. Therefore, it will point to the same object employees.
- Jack is also added to the list by calling the one-argument constructor of the Employee class while the emp2 object is created.

The correct answer is e.

Output

```
Emma David Jack
```

# Answer Quiz 3

- The ArrayList of the employees of both objects emp1 and emp2 point to the same object. Therefore, the answer is the same as the previous quiz.

# Answer Exercise 1

Using a map to answer this exercise is appropriate because it maps words with a pair of a key and its value.

## EnDictionary.java

```java
import java.util.HashMap;
import java.util.Map;
import java.util.Scanner;

public class EnDictionary
{
  Map<String, String> words = new HashMap<String, String>();

  public void addWords()
  {
    words.put("Go", "Walk");
    words.put("Buy", "Purchase");
    words.put("Happy", "Pleased");
    words.put("Translate", "Interpret");
    words.put("End", "Finish");
  }
  public static void main(String[] args)
  {
    EnDictionary enDict = new EnDictionary();
    enDict.addWords();
    Scanner input = new Scanner(System.in);
    System.out.print("\nEnter a word: ");
    String key = input.nextLine();

    if(enDict.words.containsKey(key))
    {
      String value = enDict.words.get(key);
      System.out.println("Synonymous is: " + value);
    }
    else
    {
      System.out.println("The word "+key+" is not found!");
    }
    input.close();
  }
}
```

Output 1

```
Enter a word: Happy
Synonymous is: Pleased
```

Output 2

```
Enter a word: University
The word University is not found!
```

# Answer Exercise 2

In the following exercise, the method addDishes adds the standard dishes to the ArrayList dishes. The method "contains(dish)" searches for the dish that the user enters. If the dish is not found, the dish is added to the menu.

**Menu.java**

```java
import java.util.ArrayList;
import java.util.List;

public class Menu
{
  List<String> dishes = new ArrayList<String>();

  public void addDishes()
  {
    dishes.add("Rice");
    dishes.add("Pizza");
    dishes.add("Fish");
    dishes.add("Soup");
    dishes.add("Beef");
  }
  public List<String> display()
  {
    return dishes;
  }
}
```

**MainApp.java**

```java
import java.util.Scanner;

public class MainApp
{
  public static void main(String[] args)
  {
    Scanner input = new Scanner(System.in);
    Menu menu = new Menu();
    menu.addDishes();
    System.out.print("\nCurrent Menu: " + menu.display());

    System.out.print("\nAdd a dish to the menu: ");
    String dish = input.nextLine();

    if(menu.dishes.contains(dish))
    {
      System.out.print(dish + " is already on the menu.");
    }
    else
```

```
    {
      menu.dishes.add(dish);
      System.out.print(dish + " is added: " + menu.display());
    }
    input.close();
  }
}
```

## Output 1

```
Current Menu: [Rice, Pizza, Fish, Soup, Beef]
Add a dish to the menu: Pasta
Pasta is added: [Rice, Pizza, Fish, Soup, Beef, Pasta]
```

## Output 2

```
Current Menu: [Rice, Pizza, Fish, Soup, Beef]
Add a dish to the menu: Fish
Fish is already on the menu.
```

# 5. Methods

Every class in Java has members, namely, variables and methods. Variables or attributes determine the object's state, while methods determine the behavior of the objects. You can only create a practical Java class by using methods. In this chapter, different types of methods are introduced.

- A method's name in Java starts with a lowercase letter and ends with open and closed parentheses. For example: getNetSalary(), setPrice(), getPrice(). The empty parentheses indicate that no values are passed to the method.
- Each method contains a block of code enclosed by curly braces.
- Methods allow you to specify what you want to do with objects.
- To call a method, you use the object's name followed by the method's name, separated by a dot.

In the following class Person, we define the method setData(). You can call this method by creating an object of the class Person as follows:

```
Person p = new Person();
p.setData();
```

--

**Notice**

There are two types of methods: methods that return a value and methods that don't return any value.

## Methods That Don't Return Any Value

The methods that you use to set or change values don't usually return values. If the keyword void appears before the method's name, the method doesn't return any value.

With methods that don't return values, you can change or set the values of the variables. In the following example, the method setData sets the variable's name, age, and salary value. This method doesn't return any value because it begins with the keyword void.

The attribute's name, age, and salary values are not initialized in the following example. Therefore, the values are the standard in Java, respectively null, 0, and 0.0.

Once you call the method setData(), all the variables(attributes) are set to the data assigned in the method.

## *Example 1: Void Method*

**Person.java**

```java
public class Person
{
  String name;
  int age;
  double salary;

  public void setData()
  {
    this.name = "Emma";
    this.age = 21;
    this.salary = 3000.00;
  }
  public static void main(String[] args)
  {
    // before calling the method
    Person p = new Person();
    System.out.println();
    System.out.println(p.name);
    System.out.println(p.age);
    System.out.println(p.salary);
    System.out.println("--------------");
    // calling the method
    p.setData();
    // after calling the method
    System.out.println(p.name);
    System.out.println(p.age);
    System.out.println(p.salary);
  }
}
```

Output

```
null
0
0.0
-------------
Emma
21
3000.0
```

# Methods that Return Values

Methods that return value usually return a primitive variable or an object. If a variable type or an object type appears before the method's name, that method returns that variable type. The data type for the method's name is the same type variable that the method returns. In Java, the keyword return is used before the returned result. The rest of the method's body is ignored when a return statement is reached.

The method getMinutesInDay() calculates the daily minutes in the following example. Before the method's name, the int variable returns a value of the integer type.

## *Example 2: Methods that Return Values*

**Time.java**

```java
public class Time
{
  public int getMinutesInDay()
  {
    int HoursInDay = 24; // hours
    int MinutesInHour = 60; //minutes
    int minInDay = HoursInDay * MinutesInHour;
    return minInDay;
  }
  public static void main(String[] args)
  {
    Time t = new Time();
    int mInDay = t.getMinutesInDay();
    System.out.println();
    System.out.printf("Minutes in day: " + mInDay);
  }
}
```

Output

```
Minutes in day: 1440
```

## Parameters

A parameter could be a primitive variable or an object, and you can pass zero or more parameters to a method.

## *Example 3: Method Parameters*

In this example, the method getWage calculates the wage of an employee based on the years of experience. An employee who has less than two years of experience will be rejected. The base salary is $1500. An employee with
- Two years of experience gets 1500 + 1000
- Three years of experience gets 1500 + 2000
- More than three years of experience gets 1500 + 3000.

**Wage.java**

```java
public class Wage
{
  // yExperience = years of experience
  public double getWage(int yExperience)
  {
    double wage = 1500;

    if(yExperience == 2)
    {
      wage += 1000;
    }
    else if(yExperience == 3)
    {
      wage += 2000;
    }
    else if(yExperience > 3)
    {
      wage += 3000;
    }
    else
    {
      wage = 0;
    }
    return wage;
  }
  public static void main(String[] args)
```

```java
  {
    Wage wage = new Wage();
    System.out.printf("\nWage is: $%.2f ", wage.getWage(3));
  }
}
```

Output

```
Wage is: $3500.00
```

## Quiz 1: Void Method

What happens when the following code is compiled and run?

**Student.java**

```java
public class Student
{
  String name;
  int age;

  public void updateData(String name, int age)
  {
    this.name = name;
    System.out.print(" 1 ");
  }
  public static void main(String[] args)
  {
    Student st1 = new Student();
    st1.updateData("Jack", 24);
    System.out.println(st1.name + " "+ st1.age);
  }
}
```

Select the correct answer.

a. The code writes 1 Jack 0

b. The code writes 1 Jack 24

c. The code writes 1 null  0

d. The code writes  Jack 0

e. The code writes  Jack 24

f. The code writes  null 0

## *Quiz 2: Return Method Metal*

What happens when the following code is compiled and run?

**Metal.java**

```java
public class Metal
{
  public double getPrice(String metal)
  {
    double price = 15;

    if(metal.equals("GD")) //.........GD: Gold
    {
      price += 2000;
    }
    else if(metal.equals("SV")) //...SV: Silver
    {
      price += 25;
    }
    else if(metal.equals("CP")) //...CP: Copper
    {
      price += 3;
    }
    else
    {
      price -= 5;
    }
    return price;
  }
  public static void main(String[] args)
  {
    Metal m = new Metal();
    double price = m.getPrice(null);
    System.out.println(price);
  }
}
```

Select the correct answer.

a. The code writes 2015.0.

b. The code writes 40.0.

c. The code writes 10.0.

d. The code writes null.

e. The code writes 18.0.

f. The code causes error.

## *Quiz 2B: Return Method Metal*

**Metal.java**

```java
public class Metal
{
  public double getPrice(String metal)
  {
    double price = 15;

    if(metal == "GD") //........GD: Gold
    {
      price += 2000;
    }
    else if(metal == "SV") //...SV: Silver
    {
      price += 25;
    }
    else if(metal == "CP") //...CP: Copper
    {
      price += 3;
    }
    else
    {
      price -= 5;
    }
    return price;
  }
  public static void main(String[] args)
  {
    Metal m = new Metal();
    double price = m.getPrice(null);
    System.out.println(price);
  }
}
```

Select the correct answer.

a. The code writes 2015.0.

b. The code writes 40.0.

c. The code writes 10.0.

d. The code writes null.

e. The code writes 18.0.

f. The code causes error.

## *Quiz 2C: Return Method Metal*

**Metal.java**

```java
public class Metal
{
  public double getPrice(String metal)
  {
    double price = 15;

    if(metal == "GD") //........GD: Gold
    {
      price += 2000;
    }
    else if(metal == "SV") //...SV: Silver
    {
      price += 25;
    }
    else if(metal == "CP") //...CP: Copper
    {
      price += 3;
    }
    else
    {
      price -= 5;
    }
    return price;
  }
  public static void main(String[] args)
  {
    Metal m = new Metal();
    double price = m.getPrice("GD");
    System.out.println(price);
  }
}
```

Select the correct answer.

a. The code writes 2015.0.

b. The code writes 40.0.

c. The code writes 10.0.

d. The code writes null.

e. The code writes 18.0.

f. The code causes error.

# Varargs Methods

The Varargs method allows an unfixed number of arguments (parameters). The Varargs feature is introduced in Java 5.

Suppose that you need a method that creates a table. The number of columns in the table could be one, two, three, or more. In that case, you have either to write a method for each number of the parameters or write even more methods for the number of columns needed in the future.

Another solution is to add the columns to a list and pass the list as a parameter through the method.

However, Java does have a better and easier solution to pass an unfixed number of parameters through a single method. That solution is called Varargs, which means variable arguments.

## *Example 4A: Fixed Number of Columns*

In the following code, the method display creates three columns. Suppose you need one, two, three, four, and an unfixed number of columns. How do you apply that feature in the code? An option is to write a separate method for each number of columns; That option is time- and code-consuming.

Improve the code to create tables with any number of columns you need by updating the following code with minimum changes.

**Table.java**

```java
public class Table
{
  final String SIGN = "*";
  final String SPACE = "    ";

  public void display(String title1, String title2, String title3)
  {
    String titleText = "";
    String underTitle = "";
    String newLine = "\n";

    titleText += title1 + SPACE;;
    underTitle += SIGN.repeat(title1.length()) + SPACE;

    titleText += title2 + SPACE;;
    underTitle += SIGN.repeat(title2.length()) + SPACE;
```

```java
    titleText += title3 + SPACE;;
    underTitle += SIGN.repeat(title3.length()) + SPACE;

    System.out.print(titleText + SPACE + newLine);
    System.out.print(underTitle);
  }
  public static void main(String[] args)
  {
    Table tb = new Table();
    System.out.println("\n.... Three arguments ....\n");
    tb.display("Product", "Brand", "Price");
  }
}
```

Output:  Three arguments are passed through the method display

```
.... Three arguments ....

Product    Brand    Price
*******    *****    *****
```

---

## Notice

The SIGN is the character you want to use for the title underline, and the number of signs for the underline should equal the number of characters in the title.

If you change the SIGN from asterisk "*" to an equal sign "=," the output will be as follows.

```
.... Three arguments ....

Product    Brand    Price
=======    =====    =====
```

## Varargs Methods in Java

Varargs methods allow creating methods with an unfixed number of parameters.

## *Example 4B: Unfixed Number of Columns*

The easiest way to create an unfixed number of columns is to use the Java feature Varargs. By using Varargs, you can pass as many parameters through the method as you need.

**Varargs method**

```java
public void display(String... titles)
```

By invoking the method display, we can pass through the method one, two, three, four, or even an unfixed number of arguments, as shown below.
In the previous code, three arguments are passed through the method display. In the following code, different parameters are passed through the method display.

**Table.java**

```java
public class Table
{
  final String SIGN = "*";
  final String SPACE = "    ";

  public void display(String... titles)
  {
    String titleText = "";
    String underTitle = "";
    String newLine = "\n";

    for (String title : titles)
    {
      titleText += title + SPACE;;
      underTitle += SIGN.repeat(title.length()) + SPACE;
    }
    System.out.print(titleText + SPACE + newLine);
    System.out.print(underTitle);
  }
  public static void main(String[] args)
  {
    Table tb = new Table();

    System.out.println("\n.... One Column ....\n");
    tb.display("Product");

    System.out.println("\n.... Two Columns ....\n");
    tb.display("Product", "Brand");
```

```java
    System.out.println("\n.... Three Columns ....\n");
    tb.display("Product", "Brand", "Price");

    System.out.println("\n.... Four Columns ....\n");
    tb.display("Product", "Brand", "Price", "Category");

    System.out.println("\n.... Five Columns ....\n");
    tb.display("Product", "Brand", "Price", "Category", "Type");
  }
}
```

The output after improvement of the code shows that one, two, three, four, five, or more columns can be created.

```
.... One Column ....

Product
*******
.... Two Columns ....

Product    Brand
*******    *****
.... Three Columns ....

Product    Brand    Price
*******    *****    *****
.... Four Columns ....

Product    Brand    Price    Category
*******    *****    *****    ********
.... Five Columns ....

Product    Brand    Price    Category    Type
*******    *****    *****    ********    ****
```

## Varargs with multiple data types

It is also possible to use Varargs in combination with other data types.

### *Example 5: Varargs Multiple Data Types*

In the following example, people's names are categorized according to their IQ. Suppose that we need the IQ of a group of people and their names. It is not known precisely how many and which people have identical IQs. Therefore, we write a Varargs method and apply it to each group.

**IqPeople.java**

```java
public class IqPeople
{
  // varargs arguments
  void write(int iq, String... names)
  {
    System.out.print("\nIQ " + iq + ":");

    //System.out.print("Robin ");
    for (String str : names)
    {
      System.out.print(str);
    }
  }
  public static void main(String[] args)
  {
    IqPeople iqP = new IqPeople();
    // one-argument demo
    iqP.write(150);
    // two-arguments demo
    iqP.write(200, " Emma");
    // three-arguments demo
    iqP.write(220, " David", " Vera");
    // five-argument demo
    iqP.write(300, " Einstein", " Newton", " Darwin", " Tesla");
  }
}
```

Output

```
IQ 150:
IQ 200: Emma
IQ 220: David Vera
IQ 300: Einstein Newton Darwin Tesla
```

### Notice

Please note that the IQ table provided is solely for the purpose of illustrating the example code and does not reflect real-world data.

## Exercise 1: Secret Number

Write a program that allows users to guess a secret number. If the guess number equals the secret number, the program states that the number is correct, and it is terminated.

As long as the guess number is incorrect, the user is allowed to try again. The output of the program is below. As is displayed, the user tries the numbers 3, 4, and 6 and is repeatedly asked to enter a number. The program is terminated when the user enters the correct number, which is 9.

Add your code to the following program.

**Secret.java**

```java
import java.util.Scanner;

public class SecretNumber
{
  public static void main(String[] args)
  {
    int secretNumber = 9;
    Scanner input = new Scanner(System.in);

    while (true)
    {
      // insert your code here
    }
  }
}
```

Output

```
Enter a number: 3
Guess is incorrect, try again

Enter a number: 4
Guess is incorrect, try again

Enter a number: 6
Guess is incorrect, try again

Enter a number: 9
Guess number is correct
```

## *Exercise 2: Calculate Net Salary*

Write a program allowing users to enter a gross salary and tax rate. The program calculates the net salary based on the gross and tax rate.
The first time, the user enters a gross salary of $4000 and a tax rate of 0.20. The net wage calculated by the program is $3200.
The second time, the user enters a gross salary of $6000 and a tax rate of 0.50. The net wage calculated by the program is $3000.

**Salary.java**

```java
import java.util.Scanner;

public class Salary
{
  public static void main(String[] args)
  {
    Scanner input = new Scanner(System.in);
    // insert your code here
  }
}
```

Output 1

```
Enter a gross salary: $4000
Enter a taxrate %: 20
The net salary is:$3200.00
```

Output 2

```
Enter a gross salary: $6000
Enter a taxrate %: 50
The net salary is:$3000.00
```

## Answers to the Quizzes and the Exercises

## Answer Quiz 1

- In the body of the main method, the method updateData is invoked, and the parameters Jack and 24 are passed through.
- By invoking the method updateData the number 1 is written to the standard output.

- The statement this.name = name assigns the value Jack to the name of the object.
- The method doesn't assign the age to the attribute age of the object. Therefore, the standard age value, which is 0, remains.
- 

The correct answer is a. "1 Jack 0"

## Answer Quiz 2

- The parameter null is passed through the method getPrice. The if statement metal.equals("GD") tries invoking the method equals in the class String.
- If the String metal is null, you cannot invoke members attributes or methods of an object if it is null because that causes the error Null Pointer Exception.

The correct answer is f.

## Answer Quiz 2B

- The parameter null is passed through the method getPrice(null). The value 15 is assigned to the variable price.
- The if and the else if statements return false because the value null does not equal GD, SV, or CP. The else statement is executed; therefore, the price is decremented by 5. The output is 15 - 5 =10.0.

The correct answer is c.

- 

## Answer Quiz 2C

- The parameter GD is passed through the getPrice("GD") method. The value 15 is assigned to the variable price.
- The first if statement compares the metal parameter with GD, and that returns true.
- The price is incremented with 2000, so it becomes 2015.0.

The correct answer is a.

# Answer Exercise 1

We can use a loop to allow the user to enter a guess number repeatedly. In this example, I used a while loop and the true argument that guarantees the execution of the loop's body continually. As soon as the user enters a correct guess number, the break statement is reached, and the loop is terminated.

**SecretNumber.java**

```java
import java.util.Scanner;
import java.util.ArrayList;

public class SecretNumber
{
  public static void main(String[] args)
  {
    int secretNumber = 9;
    Scanner input = new Scanner(System.in);

    while (true)
    {
      System.out.print("\nEnter a number: ");
      int guessNumber = input.nextInt();

      if(guessNumber == secretNumber)
      {
        System.out.println("Guess number is correct");
        break;
      }
      else
      {
        System.out.println("Guess is incorrect, try again");
      }
    }
    input.close();
  }
}
```

Output

```
Enter a number: 7
Guess is incorrect, try again

Enter a number: 3
Guess is incorrect, try again

Enter a number: 9
Guess number is correct
```

# Answer Exercise 2

This example uses a simple calculation of a net wage based on a gross salary and tax rate. First, we allow the user to enter a gross salary and the tax rate, and based on that, we can calculate the net salary.

**Salary.java**

```java
import java.util.Scanner;

public class Salary
{
  public static void main(String[] args)
  {
    Scanner input = new Scanner(System.in);

    System.out.print("Enter a gross salary: $");
    double grossSalary = input.nextDouble();

    System.out.print("Enter a taxrate %: ");
    double taxrate = input.nextDouble();

    double totalTax = grossSalary * (taxrate / 100);
    double netSalary = grossSalary - totalTax;
    System.out.printf("The net salary is:$%.2f", netSalary);
    input.close();
  }
}
```

Output

```
Enter a gross salary: $4000
Enter a taxrate %: 20
The net salary is:$3200.00
```

# 6. Packages and Access Modifiers

The main reasons for using packages are:
- Using a class name more than once in one package is not allowed, but using the same class name is possible if they exist in different packages.
- Package and access modifiers allow more control and visibility by accessing other parts of the program.
- A package allows to categorize the classes that are logically related. For example, if you have different classes to manipulate images, you can put them in one package and reuse that package in other applications.

## Organize Your Code

Usually, a statement is at the top of a Java class, such as a "package. application".
Java classes must be saved in a file with a ".java" extension. Packages are essentially directories, and they are separated from subdirectories with a dot ".". The "import" statement is required to access classes in different packages.

```
import java.util.List;
```

## Access Modifiers

Java supports the accessibility of the classes and class members with the following keywords. All group members are accessible from classes in which they exist, regardless of their keywords.

### Public

A public class or member is accessible from any other class.

## Protected

A protected class or member is accessible from classes of the same package. You can also access protected members of a class in other packages if your class extends that class or use it as a superclass.

> **Notice**
> Subclasses and superclasses are covered in the chapter Inheritance.

## Package/ Default

Package or default modifier does not have a keyword. A package class or member is accessible only from classes and members in the same package.

## Private

A private class or member is accessible only from the class where it is defined. The following table shows the access level of the above access modifiers.

## Table 1: Access Modifiers

| Keyword | Within the Class | Within the Package | From a Subclass | Outside package |
|---|---|---|---|---|
| Public | Yes | Yes | Yes | Yes |
| default | Yes | Yes | No | No |
| protected | Yes | Yes | Yes | No |
| private | Yes | No | No | No |

> **Notice**
> To use a public class from other packages in your classes, you must import it. If you have a class defined in a different Java package, you cannot use

them without importing them.

For example, if you want to use the class ArrayList in the package java util, you need to use the following import statement in your class:

```java
import java.util.ArrayList;
```

Suppose you need to use many classes in the package java.util. You don't need to import each class separately; instead, you can use ".*" at the end of the package. This statement means you import the whole package:

```java
import java.util.*;
```

## Example 1: Packages Animals

In the following example, the classes Dog and MainApp are in two packages: package application and animal. Both classes are public, and the attribute type in Dog is also public. However, you cannot create a dog object inside the class MainApp if you do not import the package where the class Dog is.


**Dog.java**

```java
package animal;

// package animal;
public class Dog
{
   public String type = "Husky";
}
```

**MainApp.java**

```java
package application;

import animal.Dog;

// package application
public class MainApp
{
   public static void main(String[] args)
```

```java
{
    Dog dog = new Dog();
    System.out.println(dog.type);
  }
}
```

Output

```
Husky
```

## *Quiz 1: Access Modifiers Computer Class*

The class Computer is declared public and has three attributes with different access modifiers. The class MainApp is also located within the same package. Among statements 1, 2, 3 and 4 in the class MainApp, which one could cause an error?

**Computer.java**

```java
public class Computer
{
  public String brand = "IBM"; //...public access
  double price; //..................default access
  private int memory = 16; //.......private access
}
```

**MainApp.java**

```java
public class MainApp
{
  public static void main(String[] args)
  {
    Computer computer = new Computer(); //....1
    System.out.println(computer.brand); //....2
    System.out.println(computer.price); //....3
    System.out.println(computer.memory); //...4
  }
}
```

Select the correct answer.

a. The statement 1.

b. The statement 2.

c. The statement 3.

d. The statement 4.

e. The statements 3 and 4.

f. All the statements.

## Quiz 2: Access Modifiers

The class Computer is declared public and has three attributes with different access modifiers. The class MainApp is also declared public. Among statements 1, 2, 3, and 4 in the class MainApp, which one could potentially cause an error?

**Computer.java**

```java
package device;

// package device
public class Computer
{
  public String brand = "IBM"; //...public access
  double price; //.................default access
  private int memory = 16; //.......private access
}
```

**MainApp.java**

```java
package application;

// package application
public class MainApp
{
  public static void main(String[] args)
  {
    Computer computer = new Computer(); //....1
    System.out.println(computer.brand); //....2
    System.out.println(computer.price); //....3
    System.out.println(computer.memory); //...4
  }
}
```

Select the correct answer.

a. The statement 1.

b. The statement 2.

c. The statement 3.

d. The statement 4.

e. The statements 3 and 4.

f. All the statements.

## *Quiz 3: Access Modifiers*

The class Computer is declared public in the package device and has three attributes with different access modifiers. The class MainApp is also declared public in the package application. Among statements 1, 2, 3, and 4 in the class MainApp, which one could potentially cause an error?

**Computer.java**

```java
package device;

// package device
public class Computer
{
  public String brand = "IBM"; //...public access
  double price; //.................default access
  private int memory = 16; //.......private access
}
```

**MainApp.java**

```java
package application;

import device.Computer;

// package application
public class MainApp
{
  public static void main(String[] args)
  {
    Computer computer = new Computer(); //....1
    System.out.println(computer.brand); //....2
    System.out.println(computer.price); //....3
    System.out.println(computer.memory); //...4
  }
}
```

Select the correct answer.

a. The statements 1 and 2.

b. The statements 2 and 3.

c. The statements 3 and 4.

d. The statement 4.

e. The statements 3.

f. All the statements.

## *Quiz 4: Protected Access Modifier*

The class Computer is declared public within the package device. The subclass Laptop within the package application extends the superclass Computer, which of the following statements causes an error.
The critical question is whether an object computer in its subclass in another package can access its attributes, brand, and price.

**Computer.java**

```
package device;

public class Computer
{
  protected String brand;
  double price;
}
```

**Laptop.java**

```
package application;

import device.Computer;

public class Laptop extends Computer
{
  public String getBrand()
  {
    return brand;
  }
  public void printInfo()
  {
    Computer computer = new Computer(); //....1
    Laptop laptop = new Laptop(); //..........2
    System.out.println(computer.brand); //....3
    System.out.println(computer.price); //....4
    System.out.println(brand); //.............5
    System.out.println(laptop.brand); //......6
    System.out.println(laptop.price); //......7
  }
}
```

Select all the correct answers.

a. The statement 1.
b. The statement 2.
c. The statement 3.
d. The statement 4.
e. The statement 5.
f.  The statement 6.
g. The statement 7.

## Answers to the Quizzes and the Exercises

# Answer Quiz 1

The classes Computer and MainApp are in the same package; therefore, MainApp can access the Computer class.

- Statement 1 works fine.
- Statement 2 works fine; it writes "IBM" to the standard output because the brand attribute is public. Therefore, it is accessible from other classes in the same package.
- Statement 3 works fine; it writes "0.0" to the standard output because the price attribute is declared default; therefore, it is accessible from other classes in the same package.
- Statement 4 causes an error because the memory attribute is private. Therefore, it is not accessible from other classes even if they are in the same package.

The correct answer is d.

# Answer Quiz 2

The class Computer is in the package device, while the class MainApp is in the package application. So, they are in two different packages.

- The class Computer and its attributes are not accessible to the class MainApp. It must be imported to access the class Computer from the class MainApp.

The correct answer is f.

# Answer Quiz 3

The class Computer is in the package device, while the class MainApp is in the package application. This code is different from the previous one because this time, the class MainApp imports the package where the class Computer exists.

- Statement 1 works fine because the class Computer is accessible from MainApp.
- Statement 2 works fine because the brand attribute is declared public.
- Statements 3 and 4 cause errors because they are declared default and private; therefore, they are not accessible from other packages even if the class is imported.

The correct answer is c.

# Answer Quiz 4

The class Computer is in the package device, while the class Laptop is in the package application. The class Laptop imports the package where the class Computer exists.

- Statement 1 works fine because the class Computer is declared public; therefore, it is accessible from the class Laptop.
- Statement 2 works fine because you can create a laptop object within its class Laptop.
- Statement 3 causes an error because the computer brand is declared protected, making it accessible for subclasses outside the package but not for the Computer class.
- Statement 4 causes an error because the price is declared default and is not accessible outside the package.
- The statement 5 works fine because the Laptop class is a subclass of the Computer class, and it can access the protected attributes.
- The statement 6 works fine because the laptop class can access the protected attributes of its superclass.
- Statement 7 causes an error because the attribute price is declared default and, therefore, inaccessible outside the package.

The correct answers are c, d, and g.

# 7. Encapsulation

Encapsulation is one of the pillars of object-oriented programming.
Applying encapsulation offers more control of the data and attributes of the
classes by hiding their access directly. The data is hidden from other classes
to prevent unintentional mistakes. Encapsulation offers to restrict the direct
access to data and controls the visibility of it.

As mentioned earlier in this book, the concept of Object Oriented
Programming (OOP) is that objects interact and communicate. The question
is how an attribute could be helpful while not accessible in other classes.
The answer is to make it read-only, write-only, or modified based on a
specific rule.

An example is the code that restricts access to a balance of customers.

- By using the access modifier "private" for the balance, you forbid
  changing the balance without giving any details of how the balance
  is altered. The bank should know when and how the customer's
  balance is changed.

- Other classes can change the amount, but only through a public set
  method, which applies specific rules of the change.

- The following examples show that other classes can access the
  public read-only get-method.

## *Exercise 1: Bank Account*

The following code consists of two classes: the BankAccount and the
MainApp. The balance variable in the class BankAccount is not declared
"private"; therefore, the customer can withdraw any amount of money
regardless of his balance. If you declare the balance private, other classes
cannot access the balance attribute. Improve the code so that other classes
can only withdraw an amount lower than the balance.

Improve the code to check the following:

- A customer shouldn't be allowed to withdraw zero or a negative amount from his bank account.
- A customer shouldn't be allowed to withdraw an amount that exceeds his balance.
- For each transaction, the system should keep the date and time of the transaction.

## BankAccount.java

```java
public class BankAccount
{
   double balance = 3500.00;
}
```

## MainApp.java

```java
import java.util.Scanner;

public class MainApp
{
   public static void main(String[] args)
   {
      BankAccount bAccount = new BankAccount();
      System.out.printf("\nBalance is: %.2f", bAccount.balance);
      Scanner scanner = new Scanner(System.in);

      System.out.print("\nEnter a positive amount: ");
      double amount = scanner.nextDouble();

      bAccount.balance -= amount;
      System.out.printf("Balance is: %.2f ", bAccount.balance);
      scanner.close();
   }
}
```

The output shows that the customer withdraws $6000, and his balance becomes minus $-2500.

```
Balance is: $3500.00
Enter a positive amount: $6000
Balance is: $-2500.00
```

After improving the code, try to withdraw the following amounts to test the program: 6000, 0, -2000, and 2000, as shown below.

Output 1: The customer enters 6000, which exceeds his balance.

```
Balance is: $3500.00
Enter a positive amount: $6000

Insufficient balance

Balance is:          $3500.00
Transaction date: Fri Dec 22 15:11:06 CET 2023
```

Output 2: The customer enters an amount of zero.

```
Balance is: $3500.00
Enter a positive amount: $0

Transaction failed.

Balance is:          $3500.00
Transaction date: Fri Dec 22 15:11:55 CET 2023
```

Output 3: The customer enters a negative amount of -2000

```
Balance is: $3500.00
Enter a positive amount: $-2000

Transaction failed.

Balance is:          $3500.00
Transaction date: Fri Dec 22 15:12:49 CET 2023
```

Output 4: The customer enters an amount lower than his balance.

```
Balance is: $3500.00
Enter a positive amount: $2000

Balance is:          $1500.00
Transaction date: Fri Dec 22 15:13:24 CET 2023
```

## *Exercise 2: Volleyball Team*

A volleyball team is looking for young players to join their team. The new player can join the team if he meets the following requirements.

- He is 185 cm (72.9 inches) or higher.
- His age is from 18 to 25 years old.
- He must have at least two years of experience in the field.

Improve the following code to meet the following criteria.

- A player should not be accepted if he doesn't match the criteria.
- The following code shows that the class MainApp accesses all the player's attributes directly, which opens the door to mistakes. The class MainApp should only access the player's attributes through a method.

**Player.java**

```java
public class Player
{
    String name;
    int age;
    double height;
    int experience;
}
```

**PlayerApp.java**

```java
import java.util.Scanner;

public class PlayerApp
{
  public static void main(String[] args)
  {
    Scanner input = new Scanner(System.in);
    System.out.print("Enter the name: ");
    String name = input.nextLine();

    System.out.print("Enter the age: ");
    int age = input.nextInt();

    System.out.print("Enter the height in cm: ");
    double height = input.nextDouble();

    System.out.print("Enter years of experience: ");
```

```java
    int experience = input.nextInt();

    // direct access
    Player player = new Player();
    player.name = name;
    player.height = height;
    player.age = age;
    input.close();
  }
}
```

Improve the code to get the following results.

Output 1 based on the following input

```
Enter the name: David
Enter the age: 24
Enter the height in cm: 183
Enter years of experience: 5

---Player Info ---
Name: David
Age: 24
Height: 183.0
Experience: 5

---Result ---
David is rejected.
```

Output 2 based on the following input

```
Enter the name: George
Enter the age: 22
Enter the height in cm: 185
Enter years of experience: 3

---Player Info ---
Name: George
Age: 22
Height: 185.0
Experience: 3

---Result ---
George is accepted.
```

## *Exercise 3: Encapsulate List Laptops*

The following class Laptop declares the List of laptops as "private," which
is fine. A private access modifier prevents other classes from directly
changing the attributes' value. However, the class LaptopApp adds the brand
"Acer" to the List and removes the "HP" " as shown in the output.
Improve the code to make it read-only so that other classes can only display
the List but prevent them from updating it.

**Laptop.java**

```java
import java.util.ArrayList;
import java.util.List;

public class Laptop
{
  private List<String> laptops;
  {
    laptops = new ArrayList<>();
    laptops.add("Dell");
    laptops.add("IBM");
    laptops.add("HP");
    laptops.add("Lenovo");
  }
  public List<String> getListLaptops()
  {
    return laptops;
  }
}
```

**LaptopApp.java**

```java
public class LaptopApp
{
  public static void main(String[] args)
  {
    Laptop laptop = new Laptop();
    // adds the brand Acer to the list
    laptop.getListLaptops().add("Acer");
    // removes the brand with index 2 which is HP
    laptop.getListLaptops().remove(2);
    System.out.print("\n"+laptop.getListLaptops());
  }
}
```

The output clearly shows that the brand Acer is added to the list, and HP is
removed.

```
[Dell, IBM, Lenovo, Acer]
```

After improving the code, the list remains unchanged, as shown below.

```
The list is read-only.
[Dell, IBM, HP, Lenovo]
```

# Answers to the Quizzes and the Exercises

# Answer Exercise 1

- The balance attribute should be declared private to prevent direct access from outside the class BankAccount.
- Write a public method "withdraw" to meet all the requirements.
- Write a public method, "getBalance," to display the balance in other classes.

**BankAccount.java**

```java
import java.util.Date;

public class BankAccount
{
  private double balance = 3500.00;

  public void withdraw(double amount)
  {
    if(amount > 0)
    {
      if(amount <= balance)
      {
        this.balance = balance - amount;
      }
      else
      {
        System.out.println("\nInsufficient balance");
      }
    }
    else
    {
      System.out.println("\nTransaction failed.");
    }
    System.out.printf("\nBalance is:        $%.2f ", balance);
    printCurrentDate();
  }
  public void printCurrentDate()
```

```java
  {
    Date currentDate = new Date();
    System.out.println("\nTransaction date: " + currentDate);
  }
  public double getBalance()
  {
    return balance;
  }
}
```

**MainApp.java**

```java
import java.util.Scanner;

public class MainApp
{
  public static void main(String[] args)
  {
    BankAccount ba = new BankAccount();
    System.out.printf("\nBalance is: $%.2f ", ba.getBalance());

    Scanner scanner = new Scanner(System.in);
    System.out.print("\nEnter a positive amount: $");
    double amount = scanner.nextDouble();

    ba.withdraw(amount);
    scanner.close();
  }
}
```

# Answer Exercise 2

By using a conditional statement, the program can decide whether the player meets the team's requirements.

**Player.java**

```java
public class Player
{
  private String name;
  private int age;
  private double height; // in cm
  private int yEx; // years of experience

  public Player(String name, int age, double height, int yEx)
  {
    this.name = name;
    this.age = age;
    this.height = height;
```

```java
    this.yEx = yEx;
  }
  public void printAll()
  {
    System.out.println("Name: " + name);
    System.out.println("Age: " + age);
    System.out.println("Height: " + height);
    System.out.println("Experience: " + yEx);
  }
}
```

## PlayerApp.java

```java
import java.util.Scanner;

public class PlayerApp
{
  public static void main(String[] args)
  {
    Scanner input = new Scanner(System.in);

    System.out.print("\nEnter the name: ");
    String name = input.nextLine();

    System.out.print("Enter the age: ");
    int age = input.nextInt();

    System.out.print("Enter the height in cm: ");
    double height = input.nextDouble();

    System.out.print("Enter years of experience: ");
    int yEx = input.nextInt();

    Player player = new Player(name, age, height, yEx);
    System.out.println("\n---Player Info ---");
    // access through public method
    player.printAll();
    System.out.println("\n---Result ---");

    if(age >= 18 && age <= 25 && height >= 185 && yEx >= 2)
    {
      System.out.println(name + " is accepted.");
    }
    else
    {
      System.out.println(name + " is rejected.");
    }
    input.close();
  }
}
```

# Answer Exercise 3

Declaring a list private in Java indicates that the list is only accessible within that class. However, a method that returns the private list allows other classes to access a reference to the list and potentially modify its content.

This behavior is not a bug in Java but rather a consequence of how object references work in the language. By returning a reference to a list from a method, access is provided to that list object. Any changes made in that reference will change the original object.

If you want to restrict the modification access to the list within the same class, returning a copy or an unmodified list will prevent other classes from modifying it.

# Answer 1

Adding and removing elements from the list can be prevented by returning a copy of the list as follows. Replace the statement "return laptops;" with "return new ArrayList(laptops)." Let's check the output to see whether the list remains unchangeable.

**Laptop.java**

```java
import java.util.ArrayList;
import java.util.List;

public class Laptop
{
  private List<String> laptops;
  {

    laptops = new ArrayList<>();
    laptops.add("Dell");
    laptops.add("IBM");
    laptops.add("HP");
    laptops.add("Lenovo");
  }
  public List<String> getListLaptops()
  {
    return new ArrayList<String>(laptops);
  }
}
```

**LaptopApp.java**

```java
public class LaptopApp
{
  public static void main(String[] args)
  {
    Laptop laptop = new Laptop();
    // trying to add Acer to the list
    laptop.getListLaptops().add("Acer");
    // trying to remove HP from the list
    laptop.getListLaptops().remove(2);
    System.out.println("\nThe list is read-only.");
    System.out.print(laptop.getListLaptops());
  }
}
```

The output shows that the list has not changed.

```
The list is read-only.
[Dell, IBM, HP, Lenovo]
```

# Answer 2

The second solution is to return the unmodifiable list of laptops in the code, as shown below.

Returning an unmodifiable List solution is often better because sometimes you don't want to work with more list copies. That might cause unwanted results in some situations.

In this version, the original list cannot be changed. When trying to change the list, the exception "UnsupportedOperationException" occurs.

**Laptop.java**

```java
import java.util.ArrayList;
import java.util.Collections;
import java.util.List;

public class Laptop
{
  private List<String> laptops;
  {
    laptops = new ArrayList<>();
    laptops.add("Dell");
    laptops.add("IBM");
    laptops.add("HP");
```

```java
      laptops.add("Lenovo");
  }
  public List<String> getListLaptops()
  {
    return Collections.unmodifiableList(laptops);
  }
}
```

## LaptopApp.java

```java
public class LaptopApp
{
  public static void main(String[] args)
  {
    Laptop laptop = new Laptop();
    try
    {
      // trying to add Acer to the list
      laptop.getListLaptops().add("Acer");
      // trying to remove HP from the list
      laptop.getListLaptops().remove(2);
    }
    catch(UnsupportedOperationException e)
    {
      System.out.println("\nThe list is read-only.");
    }
    //  display the list after trying to change it
    System.out.print(laptop.getListLaptops());
  }
}
```

Let's check the output of the program.

```
The list is read-only.
[Dell, IBM, HP, Lenovo]
```

# 8. Inheritance

Java supports inheritance, a fundamental concept in object-oriented programming that enables code reuse and the creation of new classes by building upon existing ones. To effectively use inheritance in software design, it's crucial to understand the concepts of generalization and specialization. The following example illustrates how inheritance enhances code reusability and maintainability:

## Avoiding Redundancy

Suppose a university requires a program with three classes: Student, Professor, and MainApp, as shown in the following example.

## *Example 1: University Inheritance*

This code does not reuse attributes such as 'name' and 'email,' which are common to both students and professors. While intended to demonstrate the importance of inheritance, it must be written professionally.

**Student.java**

```java
public class Student
{
  private String name;
  private String email;
  private String group;

  public Student(String name, String email, String group)
  {
    this.name = name;
    this.email = email;
    this.group = group;
  }
  public void printData()
  {
    System.out.println("\n........ Student ........");
    System.out.println("Name:      " + name);
    System.out.println("email:     " + email);
    System.out.println("Group:     " + group);
  }
}
```

## Professor.java

```java
public class Professor
{
  private String name;
  private String email;
  private double salary;

  public Professor(String name, String email, double salary)
  {
    this.name = name;
    this.email = email;
    this.salary = salary;
  }
  public void printData()
  {
    System.out.println("\n........ Professor ........");
    System.out.println("Name:        " + name);
    System.out.println("email:       " + email);
    System.out.printf("Salary:       $%.2f", salary);
  }
}
```

## UniversityApp.java

```java
public class UniversityApp
{
  public static void main(String[] args)
  {
    Student st = new Student("Emma", "emma@mail.com", "A3");
    Professor pf = new Professor("Tim", "tim@mail.com", 5600);
    st.printData();
    pf.printData();
  }
}
```

Output

```
........ Student .......
Name:        Emma
email:       emma@mail.com
Group:       A3


........ Professor ........
Name:        Tim
email:       tim@mail.com
Salary:      $5600.00
```

The attributes 'name' and 'email' are redundant in both the Professor and Student classes. If the university requires additional information, such as email, postal address, and age, for both students and professors, adding these attributes to both classes results in duplicated effort.

We first remove 'name' and 'email' from both classes to eliminate the redundant attributes. We temporarily remove the method 'printData' in the classes as shown below for simplicity. The class 'Student' now includes the attribute 'group,' which is specific to students since professors do not have groups. The 'Professor' class has the unique attribute 'salary,' which is specific to professors, as students do not have a salary."

## Example 1B: University Inheritance

**Student.java**

```java
public class Student
{
  private String group;

  public Student(String group)
  {
    this.group = group;
  }
}
```

**Professor.java**

```java
public class Professor
{
  private double salary;

  public Professor(double salary)
  {
    this.salary = salary;
  }
}
```

To implement the attributes name and email to both classes, we use the principle of the IS-A relationship.

# The "IS-A" Relationship

In designing the relationship between classes, there are important rules to apply. One of the rules is the "IS-A" relationship. Once you discover that relationship between the classes, using inheritance becomes clear.
Since professors and students are both persons, we created a new class called Person, as shown below.

> A student is a person
> A professor is a person

The class Person becomes the superclass of both classes, Student and professor. On the other hand, the class professor and Student become the subclasses of the superclass person, and they inherit attributes and override methods of the class Person.

As shown in the code below, Java uses the keyword "extends" to allow subclasses to inherit attributes and behavior (overriding methods) from the superclass.

**Superclass**
The superclass is the class Person who holds the common attributes, names, and email of the students and the professors.

**Subclass**
The subclasses in our example are the student and the professor. The student class holds the attribute group, which belongs only to it, while the professor class holds the attribute salary, which belongs particularly to it.

## Constructor of the Superclass

The code of example 1 had an issue. We have found that we need the superclass Person in addition to the subclasses Student and Professor. In Java, the keyword "extends" is used to inherit attributes and class members from a superclass to the subclasses. As shown in the code below, the constructor of the superclass Person initializes its attributes name and email, and we can inherit it in the subclasses by using the statement

```java
super(name, email);
```

## *Example 2: Implementing Superclass Constructor*

In this example, we call (reuse) the Person's superclass constructor within the subclass's constructors, Student and Professor.

```java
super(name, email);
```

This code shows how to implement the superclass constructor. The superclass's attributes are declared as protected to allow the subclasses to access them.

**Person.java**

```java
public class Person
{
  protected String name;
  protected String email;

  Person(String name, String email)
  {
    this.name = name;
    this.email = email;
  }
}
```

**Student.java**

```java
public class Student extends Person
{
  private String group;
```

```java
  Student(String name, String email, String group)
  {
    // calls the person's constructor
    super(name, email);
    this.group = group;
  }
  public void printData()
  {
    System.out.println("\n........ Student ........");
    System.out.println("Name:        " + name);
    System.out.println("email:       " + email);
    System.out.println("Group:       " + group);
  }
}
```

## Professor.java

```java
public class Professor extends Person
{
  private double salary;

  Professor(String name, String email, double salary)
  {
    // calls the person's constructor
    super(name, email);
    this.salary = salary;
  }
  public void printData()
  {
    System.out.println("\n........ Professor ........");
    System.out.println("Name:        " + name);
    System.out.println("email:       " + email);
    System.out.printf("Salary:      $%.2f", salary);
  }
}
```

## UniversityApp.java

```java
public class UniversityApp
{
  public static void main(String[] args)
  {
    Student st = new Student("Bruce", "bruce@mail.com", "2A");
    Professor pr = new Professor("Ben", "ben@mail.com", 4500);
    st.printData();
    pr.printData();
  }
}
```

Output

```
........ Student ........
Name:          Bruce
email:         bruce@mail.com
Group:         2A


........ Professor ........
Name:          Ben
email:         ben@mail.com
Salary:        $4500.00
```

# Overriding Methods

We applied the Inheritance concept to the constructors in the code of the previous example. So, we have reused or inherited the superclass code in the subclasses. We still have the following redundant statements in the method printData.

```
System.out.println("Name: " + name);
System.out.println("email: " + email);
```

We have those statements in both classes, Student and Professor. By printing more common data of the students and professors, we need to add extra statements to both classes. To avoid this redundancy in the methods, we override the method printData in the subclasses Student and Professor. To apply that, we need to add the method printData to the superclass Person and print its attributes inside that method. Then, we can override that method in the subclasses by using the statement super(name, email);

## *Example 3: Overriding Methods*

In this example, we reuse the Person's superclass constructor within the subclass's constructors, Student and Professor. We also override the method printData of the superclass Person.

```
super.printData();
```

This code is better than the previous examples because the subclasses inherit both the constructor as well as the method of the superclass.

**Person.java**

```java
public class Person
{
  protected String name;
  protected String email;

  Person(String name, String email)
  {
    this.name = name;
    this.email = email;
  }
  public void printData()
  {
    System.out.println("Name:          " + name);
    System.out.println("email:         " + email);
  }
}
```

**Student.java**

```java
public class Student extends Person
{
  private String group;

  Student(String name, String email, String group)
  {
    // calls the person's constructor
    super(name, email);
    this.group = group;
  }
  public void printData()
  {
    System.out.println("\n........ Student ........");
    // overrides the method printData of the superclass
    super.printData();
    System.out.println("Group:         " + group);
  }
}
```

**Professor.java**

```java
public class Professor extends Person
{
  private double salary;

  Professor(String name, String email, double salary)
```

```java
  {
    // calls the person's constructor
    super(name, email);
    this.salary = salary;
  }
  public void printData()
  {
    System.out.println("\n........ Professor ........");
    // overrides the method printData of the superclass
    super.printData();
    System.out.printf("Salary:       $%.2f", salary);
  }
}
```

## UniversityApp.java

```java
public class UniversityApp
{
  public static void main(String[] args)
  {
    Student st = new Student("Bruce", "bruce@mail.com", "2A");
    Professor pr = new Professor("Ben", "ben@mail.com", 4500);

    st.printData();
    pr.printData();
  }
}
```

The previous example's code is complete, the subclasses inherit all the superclass members.

The output of the above program is.

```
........ Student ........
Name:        Bruce
email:       bruce@mail.com
Group:       2A

........ Professor ........
Name:        Ben
email:       ben@mail.com
Salary:       $4500.00
```

## *Exercise 1: Add Courses to the Professor Class*

Suppose that the university wants to expand the data they store. Therefore, they want to keep the courses that professors give and the ages of the students as well as the professors. Expand the code of Example 3 to build that feature. Avoid redundancy and reuse your code whenever possible. The expected output is shown below.

```
........ Student ........
Name:           Bruce
email:          bruce@mail.com
Age:            21
Group:          2A

........ Professor ........
Name:           Ben
email:          ben@mail.com
Age:            47
Salary:         $4500.00

Courses.....
  1: Java
  2: Python
  3: C++
```

## Multiple Inheritance

Java doesn't support multiple inheritance but only allows extending a class from only one superclass directly. However, it is possible to implement more than one interface, which is covered later in this book.

Cass A extends Class B and Class C in the following UML class diagram. This kind of relationship is not allowed in Java. However, this is possible in a few other languages like C++.

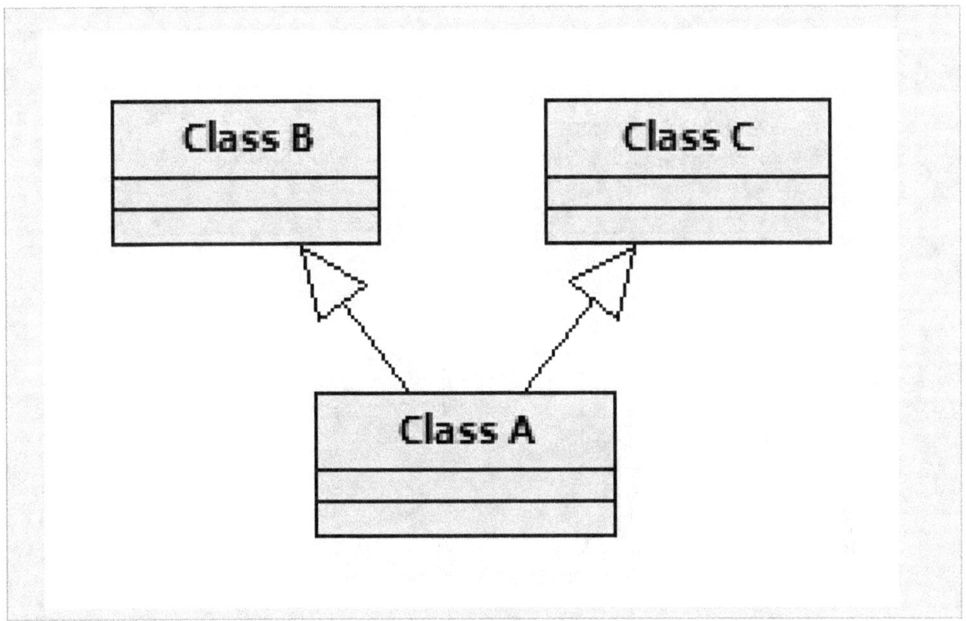


The reason that Java doesn't allow multiple inheritance is because of the ambiguity it causes. One of the common problems that occurs in numerous inheritance is the diamond problem.

## The Diamond Problem

In the following diagram, Class A extends Class B and Class C. Both mentioned classes extend Class D. Suppose a method in Class D that both classes B and C override in their way. Suppose Class A overrides the same method. Which method should class A override the method in class B or class C? That is the main reason that Java doesn't support multiple inheritance.

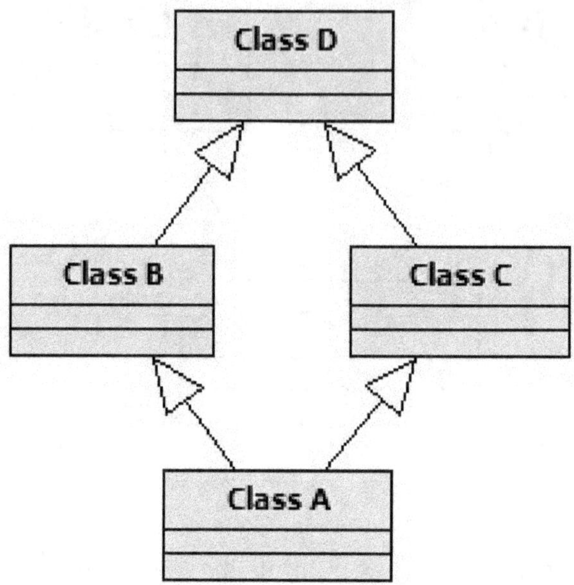


## Multilevel Inheritance

The following UML class diagram shows that Class A extends Class B and Class B extends Class C. That kind of relationship is called multilevel inheritance, supported by Java.

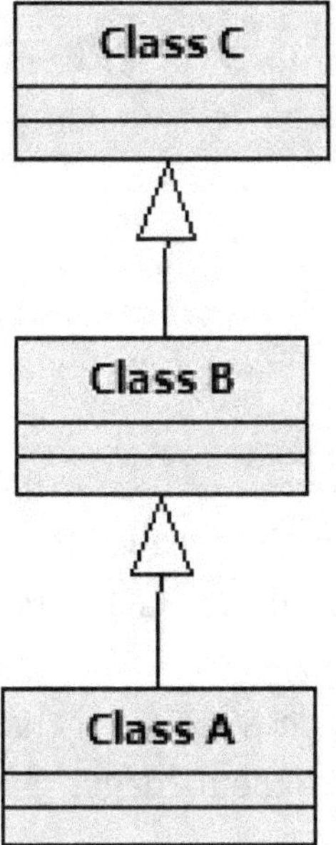


Let's apply the multilevel inheritance to our previous university example. Besides the previous data, suppose the university wants to save the attributes, name, email, salary, age, and team name managed by managers.

We use the previous table we created for the classes to apply that idea to our example. The table below shows that the managers have a common attribute of name, age, and email with the students and the professors. However, they also have a particular attribute team that they manage.

## Table 3: Multilevel Inheritance Analysis

| Student | Professor | Manager | Person |
|---------|-----------|---------|--------|
| group   | salary    | name    | name   |
|         | courses   | email   | email  |
|         |           | age     | age    |
|         |           | salary  |        |
|         |           | team    |        |

By analyzing the managers' data, we realize that managers have the attributes name, age, and email of the class Person. However, managers also have salaries like the professors.

We can simplify the table by removing the manager's attributes, such as name, age, and email, and make the manager class a subclass of the class Person, as shown below.

## Table 4: Multilevel Inheritance 2 Analysis

| Student | Professor | Manager | Person |
|---------|-----------|---------|--------|
| group   | salary    | salary  | name   |
|         | courses   | team    | email  |
|         |           |         | age    |

The question is how to eliminate the salary attribute's redundancy by the managers and professors. We can use the IS-A principle to find the common class name with the salary attribute. Only the classes Professor and Manager are involved with this issue this time. We will have the right solution if we find an appropriate name for the superclass to hold the salary attribute for the managers and the professors. Let's expand our table and try to find the name of the superclass Person.

## Table 5: Multilevel Inheritance 3 Analysis

| Student | Professor | Manager | Superclass | Person |
|---------|-----------|---------|------------|--------|

| group | subject | team | salary | name |
|-------|---------|------|--------|------|
|       |         |      |        | email |

Let's apply the IS-A principle to this situation to find an appropriate name for the Superclass.

A professor is a ---- who gets a salary.

A manager is a ----  who gets a salary.

In the above case, the word or the class name Employee is a good choice because employees have salaries. On the other hand, professors, as well as managers, are employees. An employee is also a person.

Employee IS_A person.

We replace the name Superclass with the name Employee in our table.

## Table 6: Multilevel Attributes

| Student | Professor | Manager | Employee | Person |
|---------|-----------|---------|----------|--------|
| group   | subject   | team    | salary   | name   |
|         | courses   |         |          | email  |
|         |           |         |          | age    |

We now have the names of all the classes; however, the professors and the managers must extend both classes, Employee and Person. However, we have explained that multiple inheritance is not allowed in Java.

Question: What is the solution to this situation?
Answer: We can use the concept of multilevel inheritance in this situation.

Let's apply the principle of IS-A and find out how that works!

An employee is a person.

A professor is an employee.

A manager is an employee.

In this case, the classes Professor and Manager extend their superclass Employee, and the Employee class extends its superclass Person.

## The class diagram of the application is shown below.

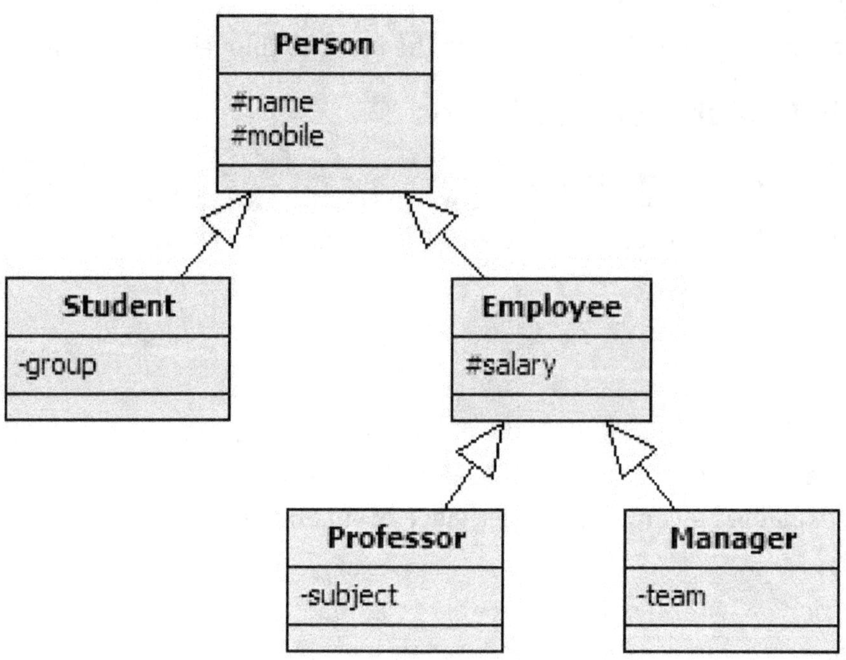


## *Exercise 2: Multilevel Inheritance University Code*

Write the complete code based on multilevel inheritance for this project using Person, Employee, Student, Professor, Manager, and the class

UniversityApp to run the program. The expected output of the program is shown below.

Output

```
----------Student-----------
Name:        Bruce
email:       bruce@mail.com
Age:         21
Group:       2A

----------Professor-----------
Name:        Ben
email:       ben@mail.com
Age:         44
Salary:      $4500.00

Provides courses.....
 1: Java
 2: Python
 3: C++

----------Manager-------------
Name:        Emma
email:       emma@mail.com
Age:         52
Salary:      $5200.00
Manages:     Team ICT
------------------------
```

## *Quiz 1: Calling the Superclass Constructor*

What happens when the following program is compiled and run?

**Publication.java**

```java
public class Publication
{
  protected String title;

  Publication(String title)
  {
    this.title = title;
    System.out.print("Java ");
  }
}
```

**Book.java**

```java
public class Book extends Publication
{
  String author;

  Book(String author)
  {
    super("Python");
    this.author = author;
  }
  public static void main(String[] args)
  {
    Book book = new Book("David ");
    System.out.print(book.title + " ");
  }
}
```

Select the correct answer.

a. This code writes "David Python" to the standard output.

b. This code writes "David Java" to the standard output.

c. This code writes "David" to the standard output.

d. This code writes "Java Python" to the standard output.

e. This code writes nothing to the standard output.

## Superclass Constructor

When an object of a subclass is instantiated, the superclass's constructor is called automatically.

## *Quiz 2: Subclass & Superclass*

What is the output of the following program?

**Publication.java**

```java
public class Publication
{
  protected String title;

  Publication()
  {
    System.out.print("PHP ");
  }
```

```java
  Publication(String title)
  {
    this.title = title;
    System.out.println("SQL ");
  }
}
```

**Book.java**

```java
public class Book extends Publication
{
  String author;

  Book(String author)
  {
    this.author = author;
    System.out.print(author);
    System.out.print("HTML ");
  }
  public static void main(String[] args)
  {
    Book book = new Book("David ");
  }
}
```

Select the correct answer.

a. This code writes "David HTML " to the standard output.

b. This code writes "PHP David HTML" to the standard output.

c. This code writes "David" to the standard output.

d. This code writes "SQL David HTML" to the standard output.

e. This code writes "HTML" to the standard output.

f. The code of the subclass causes error.

## *Quiz 3: Calling the Superclass Constructor*

What is the output of the following program?

**Publication.java**

```java
public class Publication
{
  protected String title;
```

```java
Publication(String myTitle)
{
  System.out.print(title);
  System.out.print(" Python ");
}
}
```

**Book.java**

```java
public class Book extends Publication
{
  String author;

  Book(String author)
  {
    this.author = author;
    System.out.println(author);
  }
  public static void main(String[] args)
  {
    Book book = new Book("George");
  }
}
```

Select the correct answer.

a. This code writes "null Python George" to the standard output.

b. This code writes "George" to the standard output.

c. This code writes "Python George" to the standard output.

d. This code writes nothing to the standard output.

e. The code of the subclass causes error.

## Quiz 4: Calling the Superclass Constructor

What is the output of the following program?

**Publication.java**

```java
public class Publication
{
  protected String title;

  Publication()
  {
```

```java
      System.out.print("Java ");
   }
   Publication(String myTitle)
   {
      System.out.print(title);
      System.out.print(" Python ");
   }
}
```

**Book.java**

```java
public class Book extends Publication
{
   String author;

   Book(String author)
   {
      super("C++");
      this.author = author;
      System.out.println(author);
   }
   public static void main(String[] args)
   {
      Book book = new Book("George");
   }
}
```

Select the correct answer.

a. This code writes "null Python George" to the standard output.

b. This code writes "Java C++ George" to the standard output.

c. This code writes "C++ George" to the standard output.

d. This code writes "C++ Python George" to the standard output.

e. The code of the subclass causes error.

## Answers to the Quizzes and the Exercises

# Answer Quiz 1

- In the body of the main method, the object book is created, which calls the constructor of the superclass Publication.

- In the superclass constructor's body, the value of the argument title is assigned to the attribute title.

- Further, the word Java is printed.
- The second statement in the book constructor assigns the value of the argument author to the attribute author.
- The statement Book book = new Book("David"); writes only Java to the standard output. The argument "David" is only assigned to the attribute author.
- The second statement in the body of the main method prints the book's title, "Python." Therefore, the code writes Java Python to the standard output.

The correct answer is d.

## Answer Quiz 2

- The subclass book is instantiated within the body of the main method.
- The constructor of the subclass Book doesn't call the superclass constructor directly. Therefore, the no-argument constructor of the superclass Publication is called, which prints PHP to the standard output.
- The statement System.out.print(author) prints the argument David, which is passed to the book's constructor.
- The following statement prints HTML to the standard output.

The correct answer is b.

## Answer Quiz 3

- This code causes an error because the subclass doesn't call the one-argument constructor of the superclass.
- You can solve the issue by adding a no-argument constructor to the superclass or calling the on-argument constructor in the constructor's body of the Book, as shown below.

## Answer 1

```
Book(String author)
```

```
{
    super(""); // calling the superclass constructor
    this.author = author;
    System.out.println(author);
}
```

## Answer 2

```
Book(String author)
{
    super("Learn Java"); // the one-arg superclass constructor
    this.author = author;
    System.out.println(author);
}
```

# Answer Quiz 4

- The one-argument constructor of the superclass is called first by instantiating the book class within the main method.

- The argument myTitle is not assigned to the title attribute. Therefore, the title remains null. The standard value of objects in Java is null.

- The following statement prints Python to the standard output.

- The code execution goes back to the constructor's body of the subclass, which assigns the argument value of the author to the attribute author.

- In the next step, the value of the author is printed to the standard output.

The correct answer is a.

# Answer Exercise 1

We constructed a table listing the classes and their attributes to address the exercise. The new attribute 'age' is a general attribute shared among all classes and belongs to the superclass. Consequently, we added 'age' to the 'Person' class, as illustrated in the table below. On the other hand, the new attribute 'courses' is specific to professors, so we included it in the

'Professor' class. It's worth noting that a professor may give one or more courses, leading us to use a list to represent the course attribute.

## Table 7: General and Special Attributes

| Student | Professor | Person |
|---------|-----------|--------|
| group | salary | name |
| | courses | email |
| | | age |

Here below is the code that supports saving the new data.

**Person.java**

```java
public class Person
{
  protected String name;
  protected String email;
  protected int age;

  Person(String name, String email, int age)
  {
    this.name = name;
    this.email = email;
    this.age = age;
  }
  public void printData()
  {
    System.out.println("Name:       " + name);
    System.out.println("email:      " + email);
    System.out.println("Age:        " + age);
  }
}
```

**Professor.java**

```java
import java.util.ArrayList;

public class Professor extends Person
{
  private double salary;
  private ArrayList<String> courses;

  Professor(String name, String email, int age, double salary)
  {
    // calls the person's constructor
    super(name, email, age);
    this.salary = salary;
```

```java
      this.courses = new ArrayList<String>();
   }
   public void addCourse(String course)
   {
      courses.add(course);
   }
   public void insertCourses()
   {
      courses.add("Java");
      courses.add("Python");
      courses.add("C++");
   }
   public void printCourses()
   {
      int i = 0;

      for (String course : courses)
      {
         i++;
         System.out.println(" " + i + ": " + course);
      }
   }
   public void printData()
   {
      System.out.println("\n........ Professor ........");
      // overrides the method printData of the superclass
      super.printData();
      System.out.printf("Salary:      $%.2f", salary);
      System.out.println("\n\nCourses.....");
      printCourses();
   }
}
```

## Student.java

```java
public class Student extends Person
{
   private String group;

   Student(String name, String email, int age, String group)
   {
      // calls the person's constructor
      super(name, email, age);
      this.group = group;
   }
   public void printData()
   {
      System.out.println("\n........ Student ........");
      // overrides the method printData of the superclass
      super.printData();
      System.out.println("Group:      " + group);
   }
```

```java
}
```

**UniversityApp.java**

```java
public class UniversityApp
{
  public static void main(String[] args)
  {
    Student st = new Student("Bruce", "bruce@mail.com", 21, "2A");
    Professor pr = new Professor("Ben", "ben@mail.com", 47, 4500);
    // add courses
    pr.insertCourses();
    st.printData();
    pr.printData();
  }
}
```

Output of the program is.

```
........ Student .......
Name:          Bruce
email:         bruce@mail.com
Age:           21
Group:         2A

........ Professor ........
Name:          Ben
email:         ben@mail.com
Age:           47
Salary:        $4500.00

Courses.....
 1: Java
 2: Python
 3: C++
```

# Answer Exercise 2

**Person.java**

```java
public class Person
{
  protected String name;
```

```
  protected String email;
  protected int age;

  Person(String name, String email, int age)
  {
    this.name = name;
    this.email = email;
    this.age = age;
  }
  public void printData()
  {
    System.out.println("Name:      " + name);
    System.out.println("email:     " + email);
    System.out.println("Age:       " + age);
  }
}
```

## Employee.java

```java
public class Employee extends Person
{
  protected double salary;

  Employee(String name, String email, int age, double salary)
  {
    // calls the person's constructor
    super(name, email, age);
    this.salary = salary;
  }
  public void printData()
  {
    // overrides the method printData of the superclass
    super.printData();
    System.out.printf("Salary:    $%.2f", salary);
  }
}
```

## Manager.java

```java
public class Manager extends Employee
{
  private String team;

  Manager(String name,String email,int age,double salary,String
                                                          team)
  {
    // calls the employee's constructor
    super(name, email, age, salary);
    this.team = team;
  }
  public void printData()
```

```java
    {
      System.out.println("\n----------Manager-------------");
      // overrides the method printData of the superclass
      super.printData();
      System.out.println("\nManages:    " + team);
      System.out.println("------------------------");
    }
}
```

**Professor.java**

```java
import java.util.ArrayList;

import java.util.ArrayList;

public class Professor extends Employee
{
  private ArrayList<String> courses;

  Professor(String name, String email, int age, double salary)
  {
    // calls the employee's constructor
    super(name, email, age, salary);
    this.courses = new ArrayList<String>();
  }
  public void addCourse(String course)
  {
    courses.add(course);
  }
  public void insertCourses()
  {
    courses.add("Java");
    courses.add("Python");
    courses.add("C++");
  }
  public void printCourses()
  {
    int i = 0;

    for (String course : courses)
    {
      i++;
      System.out.println(" " + i + ": " + course);
    }
  }
  public void printData()
  {
    System.out.println("\n---------Professor-----------");
    // overrides the method printData of the superclass
    super.printData();
    System.out.println("\n\nProvides courses.....");
    printCourses();
```

```
  }
}
```

## Student.java

```java
public class Student extends Person
{
  private String group;

  Student(String name, String email, int age, String group)
  {
    // calls the person's constructor
    super(name, email, age);
    this.group = group;
  }
  public void printData()
  {
    System.out.println("\n---------Student-----------");
    // overrides the method printData of the superclass
    super.printData();
    System.out.println("Group:      " + group);
  }
}
```

## UniversityApp.java

```java
public class UniversityApp
{
  public static void main(String[] args)
  {
    Student st = new Student("Bruce", "bruce@mail.com", 21, "2A");
    Professor pr = new Professor("Ben", "ben@mail.com", 44, 4500);
    pr.insertCourses();
    Manager mg = new Manager("Emma", "emma@mail.com",
                          52, 5200, "Team ICT");
    st.printData();
    pr.printData();
    mg.printData();
  }
}
```

## Output

```
---------Student-----------
Name:      Bruce
email:     bruce@mail.com
Age:       21
Group:     2A
```

```
---------Professor-----------
Name:        Ben
email:       ben@mail.com
Age:         44
Salary:      $4500.00

Provides courses.....
 1: Java
 2: Python
 3: C++

----------Manager------------
Name:        Emma
email:       emma@mail.com
Age:         52
Salary:      $5200.00
Manages:     Team ICT
-----------------------
```

# 9. Polymorphism

Polymorphism is one of the essential concepts in object-oriented programming, primarily concerning handling an object's behaviors. Two crucial terms need to be grasped to understand polymorphism: overriding and overloading methods.

## Overriding Methods

Overriding methods is the ability of a subclass to inherit behaviors of the superclass or implement a method already written in its superclass. The Inheritance chapter presents how the subclasses Student and Teacher override the method print data in the superclass.
Some rules apply to method overriding.

- The overriding method has the same name as the name of the inherited method.
- The overriding method has the same number and types of parameters as the inherited method.
- The overriding method has the same return or covariant type as the inherited method.
- The overriding method's access level must maintain the inherited method's visibility in the superclass. If the superclass method is declared public, it is not allowed to declare the overriding method private, protected, or default.

In the following example, the subclass Laptop overrides the method getSpecification in the superclass Computer.
We can use the following statement by overriding the method getSpecification in the subclass.
super.getSpeicfication(); as shown in the code

## *Example 1: Overriding Methods*

### Computer.java

```java
public class Computer
{
  String brand;
  double price;

  public Computer(String brand, double price)
  {
    this.brand = brand;
    this.price = price;
  }
  public void getSpecification()
  {
    System.out.println("Brand: " + brand);
    System.out.println("Price: $" + price);
  }
}
```

### Laptop.java

```java
public class Laptop extends Computer
{
  int screenSize;

  public Laptop(String brand, double price, int screenSize)
  {
    super(brand, price);
    this.screenSize = screenSize;
  }
  public void getSpecification()
  {
    System.out.println("\n----- Laptop -----");
    super.getSpecification();
    System.out.println("Screen size: " + screenSize + " inch");
  }
}
```

### MainApp.java

```java
public class MainApp
{
  public static void main(String[] args)
  {
    Laptop laptop = new Laptop("HP", 680.35, 17);
    laptop.getSpecification();
```

```
    }
}
```

Output

```
----- Laptop -----
Brand: HP
Price: $680.35
Screen size: 17 inch
```

# Overloading Methods

Overloading of methods is the possibility of reusing the same method name in a class as often as needed. To overload a method, the method should comply with the following requirements:

- The methods can have the same name but with a different number of parameters, such as the following method: getNetSalary.

- double getNetSalary()
- double getNetSalary(double grossSalary)
- double getNetSalary(double grossSalary, int taxRate)

- The methods can have the same number of parameters, but their parameters may not have the same data types. Below is the method name getNetSalary reused, and that is correct because the data types of the parameters are different.

- double getNetSalary(double grossSalary)
- double getNetSalary(int taxRate)

- The methods can have the same number of parameters and the same data types, provided that the order of the parameters variable type is different.

- double getNetSalary(double grossSalary, int taxRate)

- double getNetSalary(int taxRate, double grossSalary)

---

**Notice**

Two methods do not have the requirements of overloading methods if they have the same type and number of parameters but with different return types.

---

The following two methods don't have the requirements of overloading methods.

int getNetSalary (double grossSalary)

double getNetSalary (double grossSalary)

## *Example 2: Overloading Methods*

**Employee**

```java
public class Employee
{
  public double netWage()
  {
    double netWg = 3000 - (3000 * 30) / 100;
    return netWg;
  }
  public double netWage(double grossWage)
  {
    double netWg = (grossWage * 30) / 100;
    return netWg;
  }
  public double netWage(double grossWage, int taxRate)
  {
    double netWg = grossWage - (grossWage * taxRate) / 100;
    return netWg;
  }
  public static void main(String[] args)
  {
    Employee e = new Employee();
    System.out.printf("\nNet wage: $%.2f", e.netWage());
    System.out.printf("\nNet wage: $%.2f", e.netWage(2500.65));
    System.out.printf("\nNet wage: $%.2f", e.netWage(2000.0, 35));
  }
}
```

Output

```
Net wage: $2100.00
Net wage: $750.20
Net wage: $1300.00
```

# Casting Objects

Casting objects involves converting them from one type to another. In Java, implicit casting to larger data types is allowed, while casting to smaller data types must be done explicitly. It is possible to cast both objects and primitive variable types. Two kinds of casting exist: upcasting and downcasting. Java permits casting between related objects based on their positions in the class hierarchy.

# Upcasting

According to the rules of casting, you can always put an object into a more general type. So, you can implicitly cast up the hierarchy.

A subclass is always a superclass, while a superclass is not always a subclass.
A student is always a person, while a person is not always a student.
The statement in the following example is valid because Sub extends Super.
The Sub object created by the new Sub() must also be a Super object.

```
Super mySuper = new Sub();
```

--

**Notice**

By upcasting, the variable depends on the type of the object reference mySuper, while the method depends on the type of the created object.

--

> **Notice**
>
> A simple way to think about it is that a subclass does have access to all the members of the superclass, while a superclass doesn't necessarily access the details of the subclass.

## *Example 3A: Upcasting Objects*

**Super.java**

```java
public class Super
{
  int age = 100;

  public String display()
  {
    return "Super method ";
  }
}
```

**Sub.java**

```java
public class Sub extends Super
{
  int age = 50;

  public String display()
  {
    return "Sub method ";
  }
  public static void main(String[] args)
  {
    Super mySuper = new Sub();
    System.out.println("mySuper.display(): " + mySuper.display());
    System.out.print("mySuper.age:        " + mySuper.age);
  }
}
```

Output

```
mySuper.display(): Sub method
mySuper.age:       100
```

# Downcasting

If you try to cast the other way, you get the error that you cannot convert from Super to Sub.

```java
Sub mySub = new Super();
```

By downcasting, explicit casting is required.

```java
Super mySuper = new Sub();
Sub mySub = (Sub) mySuper;
```

## *Example 3B: Downcasting Objects*

**Super.java**

```java
public class Super
{
  int age = 100;

  public String display()
  {
    return "Super method ";
  }
}
```

**Sub.java**

```java
public class Sub extends Super
{
  int age = 50;

  public String display()
  {
    return "Sub method ";
  }
  public static void main(String[] args)
  {
    Super mySuper = new Sub();
    Sub mySub = (Sub) mySuper;
    System.out.println("mySuper.display(): " + mySub.display());
    System.out.print("mySuper.age:       " + mySub.age);
  }
}
```

Output

```
mySuper.display(): Sub method
mySuper.age:       50
```

## A List of the Same Type Objects

In our previous example of the chapter Inheritance, we have chosen Person as a superclass of the subclasses Student and Professor in the program's design.

Suppose the university has an application in which professors and students have different access levels. For example, professors can upload teaching materials and determine the student's grades. However, the students can only display and download the teaching materials.

Once a user logs in to the system, we need to review a list of the users to determine whether the user exists.

Creating two arrays for the students and professors is impractical because we must search in both lists until we find the user.

Adding all the students, professors, and other staff members to one list saves time and achieves that with less code.

The way to do that is to create a Java list for Person.

```java
List<Person> persons = new ArrayList<Person>();

Person student = new Student("Boris");
Person professor = new Professor("David");

persons.add(student);
persons.add(professor);
```

Since students and professors are persons, the list accepts adding both of them to it. If you make a list for the student-type objects, you cannot add professors, as shown below.

If you don't define any types of objects for the list, that would open the door for unrelated objects to be added to the list.

```java
List<Student> persons = new ArrayList<Student>();

Student student = new Student("Boris");
Professor professor = new Professor("David");

persons.add(student);
persons.add(professor); // professor can not be added
```

# *Example 4: Casting Objects*

## Person.java

```java
public class Person
{
  String name;
  String access = "Guest access";

  public Person(String name, String access)
  {
    this.name = name;
    this.access = access;
  }
  public void getAccess()
  {
    System.out.println(name + ", person : " + access);
  }
}
```

## Professor.java

```java
public class Professor extends Person
{
  public Professor(String name)
  {
    super(name, "Admin access");
  }
  public void getAccess()
  {
    System.out.println(name + ", professor: " + access);
  }
}
```

**Student.java**

```java
public class Student extends Person
{
  public Student(String name)
  {
    super(name, "Basic access");
  }
  public void getAccess()
  {
    System.out.println("\n"+name + ", student:    " + access);
  }
}
```

**MainApp.java**

```java
import java.util.ArrayList;
import java.util.List;

public class MainApp
{
  public static void main(String[] args)
  {
    List<Person> persons = new ArrayList<Person>();

    Student student = new Student("Boris");
    Professor professor = new Professor("David");

    persons.add(student);
    persons.add(professor);

    for (Person person : persons)
    {
      person.getAccess();
    }
  }
}
```

Output

```
Boris, student:    Basic access
David, professor: Admin access
```

## *Quiz 1A: Overriding and Casting*

The following code is not implemented correctly but rather to show the
reader what happens by casting a subclass and a superclass.

What is your expectation of the output of the following code?

**Person.java**

```java
public class Person
{
  protected String name = "Brian";

  public String getName()
  {
    return "Vera";
  }
}
```

**Student.java**

```java
public class Student extends Person
{
  String name = "Emma";

  public String getName()
  {
    return "Olivia";
  }
  public static void main(String[] args)
  {
    Person person = new Student();
    System.out.println(person.name + " " + person.getName());
  }
}
```

Select the correct answer.

a. This code writes "Brian Vera" to the standard output.

b. This code writes "Brian Olivia" to the standard output.

c. This code writes "Brian null" to the standard output.

d. This code writes "Emma Olivia" to the standard output.

e. This code writes "Emma Vera" to the standard output.

f. This code writes nothing to the standard output.

## *Quiz 1B: Overriding Casting*

The following code is not implemented correctly but rather to show the reader what happens by casting a subclass and a superclass.

What is your expectation of the output of the following code?

**Person.java**

```java
public class Person
{
  protected String name = "Brian";

  public String getName()
  {
    return "Vera";
  }
}
```

**Student.java**

```java
public class Student extends Person
{
  String name = "Emma";

  public String getName()
  {
    return "Olivia";
  }
  public static void main(String[] args)
  {
    Person person = new Student();
    Student student = (Student) person;
    System.out.println(student.name + " " + person.getName());
  }
}
```

Select the correct answer.

a. This code writes "Brian Vera" to the standard output.

b. This code writes "Brian Olivia" to the standard output.

c. This code writes "Brian null" to the standard output.

d. This code writes "Emma Olivia" to the standard output.

e. This code writes "Emma Vera" to the standard output.

f. This code writes nothing to the standard output.

# Example 5: Overriding Methods by Casting

The subclass student overrides the method of the superclass person. In this example, we try to invoke the method printData for both objects, person, and student object.

What is your expectation of the output of the following code?

**Person.java**

```java
public class Person
{
  protected String name = "Brian";
  protected String mobile = "088-8888";

  public void printData()
  {
    System.out.println("\n.. printData person ..");
    System.out.println("Name:     " + name);
    System.out.println("Mobile:   " + mobile);
  }
}
```

**Student.java**

```java
public class Student extends Person
{
  private String group = "ICT 2A";

  public void printData()
  {
    System.out.println("\n.. printData student ..");
    System.out.println("Name:     " + "Emma");
    System.out.println("Mobile:   " + "099-9999");
    System.out.println("Group:    " + group);
  }
  public static void main(String[] args)
  {
    Person person = new Student();
    Student student = (Student) person;
    // calling the method printData
    person.printData();
    student.printData();
  }
}
```

Output

```
.. printData student ..
Name:     Emma
```

```
Mobile:  099-9999
Group:   ICT 2A

.. printData student ..
Name:    Emma
Mobile:  099-9999
Group:   ICT 2A
```

## Explanation

The output shows that no matter which cast object, person, or student you use, both invoke the overridden method printData in the subclass.

```java
Person person = new Student();
Student student = (Student) person;
// calling the method printData
person.printData();
student.printData();
```

## *Quiz 2: Calling Methods Within Constructor*

What happens when you try to compile and run the following program?

**Person.java**

```java
public class Person
{
  String name = "Robert ";

  public Person()
  {
    printName();
  }
  void printName()
  {
    System.out.print(name);
  }
}
```

**Freelancer.java**

```java
public class Freelancer extends Person
{
  String name = "Emma ";

  void printName()
```

```
  {
    System.out.print(name);
  }
  public static void main(String[] args)
  {
    Freelancer freelancer = new Freelancer();
  }
}
```

Select the correct answer.

a. This code writes "Robert" to the standard output.

b. This code writes "Emma" to the standard output.

c. This code writes "Emma Robert" to the standard output.

d. This code writes "Robert Emma" to the standard output.

e. This code writes nothing to the standard output.

f. This code writes "null" to the standard output.

## Answers to the Quizzes and the Exercises

## Answer Quiz 1A

- The person object prints its attributes but calls the overridden method in the subclass.

The correct answer is b.

## Answer Quiz 1B

- The student object prints the attributes of the Student class and invokes the overridden method in the subclass.

The correct answer is d.

## Answer Quiz 2

Calling the overridden method printName within the constructor of the superclass person can lead to unexpected behavior, mainly if the overridden method in the subclass depends on the subclass's state, which might not be fully initialized at the time the superclass constructor is executed.

Generally, it is essential to only call overridden methods in constructors if you carefully handle potential issues related to state initialization.

- By creating the freelancer object in the main method, the superclass Person's constructor is called.
- The constructor of the class Person invokes the method printName.
- The method printName is overridden in the subclass Freelancer.
- The method printName writes the name's value to the standard output, which would be initialized after the superclass's constructor.
- Therefore, the null is printed to the standard output.

The correct answer is f.

If you add a static keyword to the name in the subclass, as shown below, the name Emma is written to the standard output. That is because the static members are initialized earlier.

**Freelancer.java**

```java
public class Freelancer extends Person
{
  static String name = "Emma ";

  void printName()
  {
    System.out.print(name);
  }
  public static void main(String[] args)
  {
    Freelancer freelancer = new Freelancer();
  }
}
```

Output

```
Emma
```

# 10. Abstract Classes, Interfaces & Enum

An abstract class is a class in which one or more methods are abstract. All abstract classes and methods are marked with the "abstract" keyword. An abstract method has no body and is not defined, only declared. In the following example, the method "getArea" is abstract; therefore, it has no body:

```
protected abstract double getArea();
```

An abstract class cannot be instantiated because it is incomplete. A subclass of an abstract class must override all its abstract methods; otherwise, it cannot be instantiated either.

## Abstract Classes and Methods

**Several concepts are essential for understanding abstract classes and methods:**

- Abstract classes cannot be instantiated because they are incomplete.
- The primary purpose of abstract classes is to use them as superclasses and override their methods.
- When a class contains one or more abstract methods, it should be declared abstract.
- An abstract method does not have a body.
- A class can be declared abstract even if it does not contain abstract methods.

# Subclasses of Abstract Classes

Subclasses of an abstract class must override all the abstract methods of their superclass; otherwise, they should also be declared abstract. It is possible to instantiate an abstract class subclass that overrides all its superclass's abstract methods. A subclass of an abstract class can also be declared abstract.

# Example of Abstract Classes

Using an example will help to understand the usage of abstract classes. Suppose a company compares mortgage packages and calculates the most desirable mortgages for its customers.
Suppose that the Rosa bank has already been added to the system.

- Rosa Bank pays three years' gross annual salary plus an extra 10% of the asset estimate value the customer already owns.

In the following example, the customer's annual salary is $36,000, and the value of his assets that he already owns is $40,000.
The method getMortgage calculates the maximum amount that the customer receives.

## *Example 1: Mortgage Class*

**RosaMortgage.java**

```java
public class RosaMortgage
{
  private double annualIncome;
  private double assetValue;

  public RosaMortgage(double anIncome, double asValue)
  {
    annualIncome = anIncome;
    assetValue = asValue;
  }
  public double getMortgage()
  {
```

```java
      double mortgage = 3 * annualIncome;
      double assetPercentage = assetValue * 0.15;
      double result = mortgage + assetPercentage;
      return result;
   }
}
```

**MainApp.java**

```java
public class MainApp
{
  public static void main(String[] args)
  {
    RosaMortgage rosaM = new RosaMortgage(36000, 40000);
    double mortgage = rosaM.getMortgage();

    System.out.printf("\nMortgage RosaBank: $%.2f", mortgage);
  }
}
```

Output

```
Mortgage RosaBank: $114000.00
```

Since the system compares mortgage packages, we need to add as many banks that offer mortgages to the system as possible. This time, we add the mortgage package by the Micro Bank to the system.

-   The Micro Bank pays only four years of gross annual salary.

The following code represents the mortgage rules that Micro Bank applies. Here, we also need a method that calculates the maximum mortgage the bank Micro offers based on their rules.

## *Example 2: Mortgage Class*

**MicroMortgage.java**

```java
public class MicroMortgage
{
  private double annualIncome;
```

```java
  public MicroMortgage(double annualIncome)
  {
    this.annualIncome = annualIncome;
  }
  public double calculateMort()
  {
    double mortgage = 4 * annualIncome;
    return mortgage;
  }
}
```

## MainApp.java

```java
public class MainApp
{
  public static void main(String[] args)
  {
    MicroMortgage microM = new MicroMortgage(36000);
    double MicroBank = microM.calculateMort();

    System.out.printf("\nMortgage MicroBank: $%.2f", MicroBank);
  }
}
```

Output

```
Mortgage MicroBank: $144000.00
```

The code works fine, but the programmer uses **calculateMort** for the
method instead of **getMortgage**, which is used in the first class. Adding
hundreds of banks and having each programmer choose different names for
the same behavior will result in an unorganized system.
In this example, we expect to add many related mortgage package classes.
Therefore, it is essential to organize it and create some rules for all the
programmers who are working with the system.

We can use abstract superclasses in object-oriented programming to enforce
developers applying specific rules.

To find the name of the abstract superclass, we use the same rule of IS-A,
which we have already used in the chapter inheritance.

## Table 1: Organize Code

| Mortgage RosaBank | Mortgage MicroBank | Superclass |
| --- | --- | --- |
| getMortgage | getMortgage | getMortgage |
|  |  |  |

Mortgage RosaBank **Is-A** Mortgage.
Mortgage MicroBank **Is-A** Mortgage.

We can replace the name of the superclass with "Mortgage." Since the class Mortgage is a general name and does not belong to a specific bank, we cannot calculate its mortgage. Therefore, we declare the method getMortgage abstract without defining its body, as shown below.

From the start, we know that our system will be highly expanded. For each bank, we have to apply its rules to calculate the mortgage it offers, but we don't necessarily need to use different names for the methods that calculate the same thing.

## *Example 3: Abstract Mortgage Class*

In this example, we apply the rules of two banks for the same customer to find out which one offers a higher amount of capital.

- The annual income of the customer is $36,000.
- He already owns an asset that has an estimated value of $40,000. The program calculates both offers of the two banks, and it is evident that the bank Micro offers more loans than the bank Rosa.

The expected output of the program is:

```
Mortgage RB: $115500.00
Mortgage MB: $144000.00
```

**Mortgage.java**

```java
public abstract class Mortgage
{
```

```java
  public abstract double getMortgage();
}
```

## RosaMortgage.java

```java
public class RosaMortgage extends Mortgage
{
  private double annualIncome;
  private double assetValue;

  public RosaMortgage(double anIncome, double asValue)
  {
    annualIncome = anIncome;
    assetValue = asValue;
  }
  public double getMortgage()
  {
    double mortgage = 3 * annualIncome;
    double assetPercentage = assetValue * 0.15;
    double result = mortgage + assetPercentage;
    return result;
  }
}
```

## MicroMortgage.java

```java
public class MicroMortgage extends Mortgage
{
  private double annualIncome;

  public MicroMortgage(double annualIncome)
  {
    this.annualIncome = annualIncome;
  }
  public double getMortgage()
  {
    double mortgage = 4 * annualIncome;
    return mortgage;
  }
}
```

## MainApp.java

```java
public class MainApp
{
  public static void main(String[] args)
  {
    RosaMortgage rosaM = new RosaMortgage(36000, 50000);
    MicroMortgage microM = new MicroMortgage(36000);

    System.out.printf("\nMortgage RB: $%.2f",
                                        rosaM.getMortgage());
```

```java
    System.out.printf("\nMortgage MB: $%.2f",
                                    microM.getMortgage());
  }
}
```

Output

```
Mortgage RB: $115500.00
Mortgage MB: $144000.00
```

To improve the code, we must provide the name of the bank that offers the mortgage. Since banks provide all the mortgages, we can declare a variable bank name inside the abstract superclass Mortgage. By doing so, all the mortgages will have access to that variable.

We expand the code as follows.

## *Example 4: Expanding Mortgage Class*

### Mortgage.java

```java
public abstract class Mortgage
{
  protected String bName;

  public Mortgage(String bName)
  {
    this.bName = bName;
  }
  public abstract double getMortgage();
}
```

### RosaMortgage.java

```java
public class RosaMortgage extends Mortgage
{
  private double annualIncome;
  private double assetValue;

  public RosaMortgage(double anIncome, double asValue)
  {
    super("Rosa Bank");
    annualIncome = anIncome;
    assetValue = asValue;
  }
  public double getMortgage()
```

```java
{
    double mortgage = 3 * annualIncome;
    double assetPercentage = assetValue * 0.15;
    double result = mortgage + assetPercentage;
    return result;
  }
}
```

## MicroMortgage.java

```java
public class MicroMortgage extends Mortgage
{
  private double annualIncome;

  public MicroMortgage(double annualIncome)
  {
    super("Micro Bank");
    this.annualIncome = annualIncome;
  }
  public double getMortgage()
  {
    double mortgage = 4 * annualIncome;
    return mortgage;
  }
}
```

## MainApp.java

```java
public class MainApp
{
  public static void main(String[] args)
  {
    RosaMortgage rm = new RosaMortgage(36000, 50000);
    MicroMortgage mm = new MicroMortgage(36000);

    System.out.printf("\n"+rm.bName+": $%.2f",rm.getMortgage());
    System.out.printf("\n"+mm.bName+": $%.2f",mm.getMortgage());
  }
}
```

Output

```
Rosa Bank: $115500.00
Micro Bank: $144000.00
```

By extending the abstract superclass, all the subclasses are enforced to override the method getMortgage and use the same name for all the methods that override it.

If a subclass of the superclass Mortgage doesn't override the method getMortgage, it should be declared abstract to avoid instantiating objects from it.


## *Exercise 1: Nano Bank App*

You have been asked to add the bank Nano bank to the system as a programmer. The mortgage rule of this bank is that they pay five annual salaries to the customer. Expand the previous example's code so that the system compares this rule with the other two banks.


The expected output of the program

```
Rosa Bank: $115500.00
Micro Bank: $144000.00
Nano Bank: $180000.00
```

# Disadvantages of Abstract Classes

In our example, we have used abstract classes because we need one or more variables belonging to all its subclasses. We can also use a constructor in abstract classes, but we cannot instantiate the class. However, we restricted the possibility that any of the subclasses to extend any other classes in the future. The reason is that Java doesn't allow multiple inheritance from classes.

In case we use multiple inheritance, we have to implement an interface.

# Interfaces

Java allows to inherit from only a single class but supports multiple inheritance from interfaces. Implementing interfaces offers a solution for objects that have various characteristics. The keyword implements is used to implement an interface. The interface's name starts as a class name with a capital letter.

## Using Interfaces

1. Subclasses that inherit a single superclass are related, but unrelated classes can implement the same interface.
2. Interfaces offer the advantage of multiple inheritance in Java.
3. Interfaces do not have constructors and cannot be instantiated.
4. Interfaces are implemented by classes using the keyword implements, but they are extended by other interfaces using the keyword extends.
5. If more than one interface is implemented, the names of the interfaces are separated by a comma.

## Interface Methods

1. All the methods in an interface are implicitly abstract.
2. A class that implements an interface must override all the methods of that interface.
3. Interface methods that are overridden by a class should be declared public.

## Interface Constants

1. By default, the constants of an interface are public, static, and final, even if no modifiers are mentioned.
2. Interface constants must be initialized.
3. It is not allowed to declare interface constants private or protected.

How do you implement an interface? In the following example, the class MyArray implements the interface List.

# Example of Interfaces

Suppose that you write a program that deals with rectangles. You write two methods to find each rectangle object's area and perimeter. The following program works fine.

The circle class has two methods to calculate the circle objects' area and perimeter. In this example, we face the same problem as the example in that we used Abstract classes. This time, we only need to organize the behavior of the classes Rectangle and Circle. Therefore, we use an interface because it offers exactly what we need without restricting the subclasses to use only one superclass.

Rectangles and circles do not have attributes in common, but they have similar behaviors or methods to calculate their area and perimeter.
We need the width and length for a rectangle, while for a circle, we need the diameter. In the table below, we have decided on the names of the methods, and now we need to force all programmers to use those names in all the subclasses that implement the same interface.

## Table 2: Name of Methods

| Rectangle | Circle | Superclass |
|---|---|---|
| getArea | getArea | |
| getPerimeter | getPerimeter | |

We use the previous IS-A principle of the inheritance chapter.

A rectangle **is a** two-dimensional shape.
A circle **is a** two-dimensional shape.

By applying the IS-A principle, we find the name Two-dimensional shape or shape is the best name we can use for the interface.

Rules that apply to the interface Shape.

- Since a shape is a general concept and it is unclear what exactly it is, we do not need to create objects of shape. An interface doesn't allow instantiation, which is not a problem.
- Every two-dimensional shape has an area and a perimeter, but how to calculate them needs to be known. Therefore, we only declare them without defining them by ignoring their bodies.
- **double getArea();**
- **double getPerimeter();**
- By implementing the interface shape, we enforce its subclasses to override the methods getArea and getPerimeter.

Once the classes Rectangle and Circle implement the interface Shape, they must override the two methods getArea and getPerimeter.

## 6. Incomplete Subclasses

Suppose that in our previous example, we must create a hexagon with six equal sides and six equal angles. Calculating the perimeter of a hexagon can be done by multiplying its side by 6. However, calculating the area is a bit complicated. If the Hexagon implements the interface Shape, it will be enforced to override both methods getArea and getPerimeter.
The following class generates an error because it overrides only the method getPerimeter of the interface Shape.

To eliminate the error, we can leave the implementation of the method getArea but declare the class Hexagon as an abstract until the method getArea is overridden.

In that way, you don't need to delete your whole code, but you prevent other programmers from instantiating objects from the class Hexagon until it is complete.

## *Example 5: Shape Interface*

### Shape.java

```java
public interface Shape
{
  public double getArea();
  public double getPerimeter();
}
```

### Rectangle.java

```java
public class Rectangle implements Shape
{
  private double width;
  private double length;

  public Rectangle(double width, double length)
  {
    this.width = width;
    this.length = length;
  }
  public double getArea()
  {
    return width * length;
  }
  public double getPerimeter()
  {
    return 2 * (width + length);
  }
}
```

### Circle.java

```java
public class Circle implements Shape
{
  private double radius;
  final double PI = 3.14;

  public Circle(double radius)
  {
    this.radius = radius;
  }
  public double getArea()
  {
    return PI * radius * radius;
  }
  public double getPerimeter()
  {
```

```
    return 2 * PI * radius;
  }
}
```

## Hexagon.java

```java
public abstract class Hexagon implements Shape
{
  double side = 5;

  public Hexagon(double side)
  {
    this.side = side;
  }
  public double getPerimeter()
  {
    return 6 * side;
  }
}
```

## MainApp.java

```java
public class MainApp
{
  public static void main(String[] args)
  {
    Rectangle rec = new Rectangle(10, 20);
    System.out.println("\n... Rectangle ...");
    System.out.printf("Area:%.2f ", rec.getArea());
    System.out.printf("\nPerimeter:%.2f",rec.getPerimeter());

    Circle circle = new Circle(20);
    System.out.println("\n... Circle ...");
    System.out.printf("Area:%.2f ", circle.getArea());
    System.out.printf("\nPerimeter:%.2f ", circle.getPerimeter());

    // you cannot instantiate the class Hexagon
  }
}
```

Output

```
... Rectangle ...
Area:200.00
Perimeter:60.00
... Circle ...
Area:1256.00
Perimeter:125.60
```

# Enum Types

An enum type is a data type used for constants such as months in the year days in the week. The fields within the enum type are usually written in uppercase because they are constants like final fields.

- The enum class body can include constructors, methods, and other fields.
- The enum constants must call the constructor, and the necessary parameters should be passed through them when the constant is defined.
- The enum constructor in Java is implicitly private, even if you do not specify it.
- The enum fields are implicitly static and final. If an enum field is declared static, a compilation error occurs.

## *Example 6: Enum Type Courses*

A university offers several courses for the next few years in the following example. Even though the courses are constant for a limited time, using an enum could be practical to avoid writing the courses everywhere in your code. This way, you can control the courses names and keep your code clean.

Adding new courses, updating or removing courses is also easier because you only need to open the enum and make the changes there.

**CourseEnum.java**

```java
public enum CourseEnum
{
  PHILOSOPHY(1, "What Is the Meaning of Life?"),
  BIOLOGY(2, "The Genius Idea of Evolution"),
  PHYSICS(3, "Einstein's Theory of Relativity"),
  HISTORY(4, "Egyptian Pyramids"),
  GEOGRAPHY(5, "The Continents"),
  TECHNOLOGY(6, "Blockchain and Cryptocurrency");
```

```java
  private final int id;
  private final String name;

  private CourseEnum(int id, String name)
  {
    this.id = id;
    this.name = name;
  }
  public int getId()
  {
    return id;
  }
  public String getName()
  {
    return name;
  }
  public String toString()
  {
    return id + ": " + name;
  }
}
```

We create a class with a main method to see how we can access the fields in our enum type.

To access the id and the course's name, we can use the name of the enum separated by a dot from the name of the course, as shown in the example. You can also access the id and the course name separately by using a method that returns their value, such as getId and getName, as shown in the following code.

### MainApp.java

```java
public class MainApp
{
  public static void main(String[] args)
  {
    System.out.println("\nCourse:  "+CourseEnum.PHYSICS);
    System.out.println("Biology: "+CourseEnum.BIOLOGY.getName());
    System.out.println("Tech id: "+CourseEnum.TECHNOLOGY.getId());
  }
}
```

Output

```
Course:  3: Einstein's Theory of Relativity
Biology: The Genius Idea of Evolution
Tech id: 6
```

## *Exercise 2: Enum Type for Messages*

In most applications, writing messages to the user is unavoidable. Many programmers write the messages directly in the code, leading to junk messages within all the classes. In this way, reusing the messages is not easy and practically time-consuming to update or improve them in the future. Rewrite the following code and put all the messages within the Registration and MainApp classes in an enum type.

**Registration.java**

```java
public class Registration
{
  private int age;

  Registration()
  {
  }
  public void setAge(int age)
  {
    if(age > 0)
    {
      if(age < 150)
      {
        this.age = age;
        System.out.println("Age is accepted.");
      }
      else
      {
        System.out.println("Age of 150+ is not allowed.");
      }
    }
    else
    {
      System.out.println("Please enter a positive number.");
    }
  }

  public int getAge()
  {
    return age;
```

```
    }
}
```

## MainApp.java

```java
import java.util.Scanner;

public class MainApp
{
  public static void main(String[] args)
  {
    Scanner input = new Scanner(System.in);
    System.out.print("Please enter your age:  ");
    int age = input.nextInt();
    Registration rg = new Registration();
    rg.setAge(age);
    input.close();
  }
}
```

Output 1

```
Please enter your age:  -33
CODE 3: Please enter a positive number.
```

Output 2

```
Please enter your age:  0
CODE 3: Please enter a positive number.
```

Output 3

```
Please enter your age:  150
CODE 2: Age of 150 + is not allowed.
```

Output 4

```
Please enter your age:  45
CODE 1: Age is accepted.
```

# Answers to the Quizzes and the Exercises

# Answer Exercise 1

**NanoBank.java**

```java
public class NanoMortgage extends Mortgage
{
  private double annualIncome;

  public NanoMortgage(double annualIncome)
  {
    super("Nano Bank");
    this.annualIncome = annualIncome;
  }
  public double getMortgage()
  {
    double mortgage = 5 * annualIncome;
    return mortgage;
  }
}
```

**MainApp.java**

```java
public class MainApp
{
  public static void main(String[] args)
  {
    RosaMortgage rm = new RosaMortgage(36000, 50000);
    MicroMortgage mm = new MicroMortgage(36000);
    NanoMortgage nm = new NanoMortgage(36000);

    System.out.printf("\n"+rm.bName+": $%.2f",rm.getMortgage());
    System.out.printf("\n"+mm.bName+": $%.2f",mm.getMortgage());
    System.out.printf("\n"+nm.bName+": $%.2f",nm.getMortgage());
  }
}
```

Output

```
Rosa Bank: $115500.00
Micro Bank: $144000.00
Nano Bank: $180000.00
```

# Answer Exercise 2

### InfoMessage.java

```java
public enum InfoEnum
{
  AGE_ACCEPTED("CODE 1", "Age is accepted."),
  AGE_150_IS_REJECTED("CODE 2", "Age of 150 + is not allowed."),
  ENTER_POSITIVE_AGE("CODE 3", "Please enter a positive number."),
  ENTER_YOUR_AGE("CODE 4", "Please enter your age:   ");

  private final String code;
  private final String message;

  private InfoEnum(String code, String message)
  {
    this.code = code;
    this.message = message;
  }
  public String getMessage()
  {
    return message;
  }
  public String getCode()
  {
    return code;
  }
  public String toString()
  {
    return code + ": " + message + "\n";
  }
}
```

### Registration.java

```java
public class Registration
{
  private int age;

  Registration()
  {
  }
  public void setAge(int age)
  {
    if(age > 0)
    {
      if(age < 150)
      {
        this.age = age;
        System.out.println(InfoEnum.AGE_ACCEPTED);
      }
      else
```

```java
        {
          System.out.println(InfoEnum.AGE_150_IS_REJECTED);
        }
      }
    else
    {
      System.out.println(InfoEnum.ENTER_POSITIVE_AGE);
    }
  }
  public int getAge()
  {
    return age;
  }
}
```

## MainApp.java

```java
import java.util.Scanner;

public class MainApp
{
  public static void main(String[] args)
  {
    Scanner input = new Scanner(System.in);
    System.out.print("\n" + InfoEnum.ENTER_YOUR_AGE.getMessage());
    int age = input.nextInt();
    Registration rg = new Registration();
    rg.setAge(age);
    input.close();
  }
}
```

# 11. Static Members and Final

## Static Members

Objects have their copy of the instance variables, but only one copy is available for all the class objects for the static variable. You can call static variables with the name of the class and the name of each instance of the class. A static variable, also called a class variable, starts with the keyword "static."

## Class Variables

Static variables are sometimes called class variables because creating objects to access the static variables is unnecessary. It is possible to access the class variables by using the name of the class without the necessity of creating objects.

## Instance Variables

Each class instance (object) has its copy of the instance variables. They are different per object.

The following code explains how the static and instance variables work.

### *Quiz 1: Instance Variables*

What happens if the following code is compiled and run?

**Item.java**

```java
public class Item
{
  String name = "";
  double price;
```

```java
  public Item(String name, double price)
  {
    this.name += name;
    this.price += price;
  }
  public static void main(String[] args)
  {
    Item item1 = new Item("Milk", 2.65);
    Item item2 = new Item("Bread", 1.85);
    Item item3 = new Item("Cheese", 2.35);
    Item item4 = new Item("Chips", 1.75);
    System.out.println(item1.name + ", " + item3.price);
  }
}
```

Select the correct answer.

a. The output of the code is "Milk, 2.65".

b. The output of the code is "Cheese, 2.35".

c. The output of the code is "Cheese, 1.75".

d. The output of the code is "Milk, 2.35".

e. The output of the code is nothing.

## *Quiz 2: Class (Static) Variables*

What happens if the following code is compiled and run?

**Item.java**

```java
public class Item
{
  static String name = "";
  static double price;

  public Item(String name, double price)
  {
    this.name += name;
    this.price += price;
  }
  public static void main(String[] args)
  {
    Item item1 = new Item("Milk ", 2.65);
    Item item2 = new Item("Bread ", 1.85);
    Item item3 = new Item("Cheese ", 2.35);
    Item item4 = new Item("Chips ", 1.75);
```

```
    System.out.println(item1.name + ", " + item3.price);
  }
}
```

Select the correct answer.

a. The output of the code is "Milk, 2.35".

b. The code output is "Milk Bread Cheese Chips, 8.6".

c. The output of the code is "Milk, 8.6".

d. The code output is "Milk Bread Cheese Chips, 2.35".

e. The output of the code is nothing.

## Quiz 3: Static ArrayList

Two instances of stores are created, namely, store A and store B storeA.addProducts adds the three products, Cheese, Milk, and Bread, to keep A while new items, Candy and Sugar, are added to store B. The loop searches for a specific item in-store A.

What happens if the following code is compiled and run?

**Item.java**

```java
public class Item
{
   String name;
   double price;

   public Item(String name, double price)
   {
      this.name = name;
      this.price = price;
   }
}
```

**Store.java**

```java
import java.util.ArrayList;

public class Store
{
   static ArrayList<Item> products = new ArrayList<Item>();
```

```java
  void addProducts()
  {
    products.add(new Item("Cheese", 3.35));
    products.add(new Item("Milk", 2.25));
    products.add(new Item("Bread", 2.25));
  }
  public static void main(String[] args)
  {
    Store storeA = new Store();
    Store storeB = new Store();

    storeA.addProducts();
    storeB.products.add(new Item("Candy", 2.55));
    storeB.products.add(new Item("Sugar", 2.55));
    int i = 0;

    for (Item item : storeB.products)
    {
      if(i == 3)
      {
        System.out.println(item.name);
      }
      i++;
    }
  }
}
```

Select the correct answer.

a. The output of the code is "Candy".

b. The output of the code is "Bread".

c. The output of the code is "Sugar".

d. The output of the code is nothing.

e. This program produced an error.

## Static Methods

There are different types of methods with similarities between them. If a method depends on objects, you must instantiate an object from the class in which it exists. However, some methods are independent of objects and could be invoked using the class name directly. Those methods are known as static methods and should be declared as static.

Examples of such methods are finding an average of numbers and calculating the sum of two or more numbers.

You can call static members with the class name, which applies to the static methods. You can call static methods with the name of the class as well as the name of the objects.

There are some essential rules which apply to static methods.

- The keyword "this" is irrelevant to be used inside static methods because "this" is associated with the current instance.
- You can not have instance variables within a static method because the instance probably does not exist when the method is called.

An example of a static method is the following, which returns the sum of three integers. This method is static because there is no need to create an object to calculate the sum of three integers. To call this method, we can also use the name of the class.

## *Example 1: Static Method*

**Calculation.java**

```java
public class Calculation
{
  public static int sum(int i, int i2, int i3)
  {
    return i + i2 + i3;
  }
}
```

**MainApp.java**

```java
public class MainApp
{
  public static void main(String[] args)
  {
    int x = Calculation.sum(5, 4, 6);
    System.out.print("Sum is: " + x);
  }
}
```

Output

```
Sum is: 15
```

Remember that not always calculating averages or sums are independent of objects. If a method calculates students' average grades, that method should not be declared static. The basic principle of that method is not just a calculation because that calculation depends on objects.
Methods dependent on objects are methods that calculate or process values that are different per object.

Let's present the idea through a piece of code. A static method calculates the average of three numbers in the math class.

## *Example 2: Static Methods Average*

**Math.java**

```java
public class Math
{
  public static double getAverage(int nr1, int nr2, int nr3)
  {
    double average = (nr1 + nr2 + nr3) / 3;
    return average;
  }
  public static void main(String[] args)
  {
    Math m1 = new Math();
    Math m2 = new Math();

    System.out.println("Avg1: " + m1.getAverage(10, 20, 30));
    System.out.println("Avg2: " + m2.getAverage(40, 60, 80));
    System.out.println("Avg3: " + Math.getAverage(45, 90, 135));
  }
}
```

Output

```
Avg1: 20.0
Avg2: 60.0
Avg3: 90.0
```

# Example 3A: Static Methods Average Grades

By calculating students' average grades, the method doesn't allow instance variables within its body.

That is because static methods are independent of objects and don't allow instance variables within their bodies. The instance variable's values are dependent on objects. If you use instance variables within the body of a static method, then you have to create the object within the body of the static method or declare each of the grades as static. Once you declare the individual grades static, the grades become the same for all the students; therefore, the average grades of all the students would be the same.
To simplify the class design and present the idea in less code, we use one class for the student and his grades as follows.

**Student.java**

```java
public class Student
{
  private String name;
  private static double gr1; // gr = grade
  private static double gr2;
  private static double gr3;

  public Student(String name, double gr1, double gr2, double gr3)
  {
    this.name = name;
    this.gr1 = gr1;
    this.gr2 = gr2;
    this.gr3 = gr3;
  }
  static double getAverage()
  {
    double average = (gr1 + gr2 + gr3) / 3;
    return average;
  }
  public static void main(String[] args)
  {
    // instance method
    Student st1 = new Student("Emma", 7, 6, 8);
    Student st2 = new Student("David", 9, 8, 7);
    Student st3 = new Student("Jack", 10, 9, 8);

    double avg1 = st1.getAverage();
    double avg2 = st2.getAverage();
    double avg3 = st3.getAverage();
```

```java
      System.out.println("Name: " +st1.name+"\tAverage: " + avg1);
      System.out.println("Name: " +st2.name+"\tAverage: " + avg2);
      System.out.println("Name: " +st3.name+"\tAverage: " + avg3);
   }
}
```

Although we passed different grades for each student through the constructor, the average grades of all the students would be the same as the last calculated average of the student, Jack, in this case.

Output

```
Name: Emma  Average: 9.0
Name: David Average: 9.0
Name: Jack  Average: 9.0
```

## *Example 3B: Instance Methods*

In the following Student class, we initialize the value of the student grades through the constructor. Once we do that, the instance method getAverage() calculates the average grades of each student individually.

To simplify the class design and present the idea in less code, we use one class for the student and his grades as follows.

**Student.java**

```java
public class Student
{
   private String name;
   private double gr1; // gr = grade
   private double gr2;
   private double gr3;

   public Student(String name, double gr1, double gr2, double gr3)
   {
      this.name = name;
      this.gr1 = gr1;
      this.gr2 = gr2;
      this.gr3 = gr3;
   }
   double getAverage()
   {
```

```java
    double average = (gr1 + gr2 + gr3) / 3;
    return average;
  }
  public static void main(String[] args)
  {
    // instance method
    Student st1 = new Student("Emma", 7, 6, 8);
    Student st2 = new Student("David", 9, 8, 7);
    Student st3 = new Student("Jack", 10, 9, 8);

    double avg1 = st1.getAverage();
    double avg2 = st2.getAverage();
    double avg3 = st3.getAverage();

    System.out.println("Name: " +st1.name+"\tAverage: " + avg1);
    System.out.println("Name: " +st2.name+"\tAverage: " + avg2);
    System.out.println("Name: " +st3.name+"\tAverage: " + avg3);
  }
}
```

Output

```
Name: Emma  Average: 7.0
Name: David Average: 8.0
Name: Jack  Average: 9.0
```

## *Quiz 4: Static Methods*

The following example clarifies that a method shouldn't be static if it
depends on objects. In the next exercise, the method that calculates the
average grade of students is declared static.

What happens if the following code is compiled and run?

**Student.java**

```java
public class Student
{
  String name;
  static double math;
  static double java;
  static double python;

  Student(String name, double math2, double java2, double python2)
  {
    this.name = name;
```

```java
    math = math2;
    java = java2;
    python = python2;
  }
  public static double getAverage()
  {
    double average = (math + java + python) / 3;
    return average;
  }
  public static void main(String[] args)
  {
    Student st1 = new Student("Jack", 8, 10, 9);
    Student st2 = new Student("Salma", 7, 9, 5);
    Student st3 = new Student("Layla", 9, 7, 8);

    double average1 = st1.getAverage();
    double average2 = st2.getAverage();
    double average3 = st3.getAverage();

    System.out.print("\nStudent name:\t" + st1.name);
    System.out.printf(" Average grade %.1f \t", average1);
    System.out.print("\nStudent name: \t" + st2.name);
    System.out.printf(" Average grade %.1f", average2);
    System.out.print("\nStudent name: \t" + st3.name);
    System.out.printf(" Average grade %.1f", average3);
  }
}
```

Select all the correct answers.

a. The average grade of Jack is "8.0".

b. The average grade of Salma is "8.0".

c. The average grade of Layla is 8.0".

d. The average grade of Jack is "9.0".

e. The average grade of Salma is "7.0".

## Quiz 5: Static Methods

In the following class, Calculator, we created a method to calculate the sum of two numbers and determine the largest number. There is no need to make any objects in this class because numbers do not depend on any objects. Therefore, we do not instantiate the class. Instead, we use the class name to use the static methods.

What is the output of the following program?

**Calculator.java**

```java
public class Calculator
{
  public static int getSum(int i1, int i2)
  {
    return i1 + i2;
  }
  public static void getLargest(int i1, int i2)
  {
    if(i1 > i2)
    {
      System.out.print(i1 + ", ");
    }
    else if(i2 > i1)
    {
      System.out.print(i2 + ", ");
    }
    else
    {
      System.out.print("equal, ");
    }
  }
}
```

**MainApp.java**

```java
public class MainApp
{
  public static void main(String[] args)
  {
    int sum = Calculator.getSum(44, -33); //...1
    System.out.print("\n"+sum + ", "); //......2
    Calculator.getLargest(24, 24); //..........3
    Calculator.getLargest(39, 41); //..........4
  }
}
```

Select the correct answer.

a. The output of the code is "11, equal, 41, ".

b. The output of the code is "44, 24, 41".

c. The output of the code is "24, 41".

d. The output of the code is "equal, 41".

e. This program produced an error.

# Final Classes & the Final Keyword

## What Is a Final Member?

The final keyword indicates that a method or a class cannot be modified or
extended.
A final variable is a constant, and its value may not be changed once it is
initialized.

## *Example 4*

In the following example, the variable HOUR is declared final. The method
convertHoursToMinutes tries to change the value of the variable HOUR,
which causes an error in the program. The reason is that a final variable is a
constant and cannot be modified once it is initialized.

**Time.java**

```java
public class Time
{
  final int HOUR = 60; // minutes

  public void converHoursToMinutes(int nrHours)
  {
    //HOUR ++;
    System.out.print(nrHours * HOUR);
  }
  public static void main(String[] args)
  {
    Time time = new Time();
    // calculate number minuts in 4 hours
    time.converHoursToMinutes(4);
  }
}
```

```
Output
240
```

# What Is a Final Class?

Declaring a class final prevents programmers from using it as a superclass. A final class in Java is a class that cannot be extended or be used as a superclass, but it can be a subclass of another class.

# What Is a Final Method?

A final method is a method that cannot be overridden in sub-classes. By declaring the method getSum final, you guarantee that the method cannot be overridden in subclasses of MyClass.

## Answers to the Quizzes and the Exercises

# Answer Quiz 1

- The code prints the name of item 1 and the price of item 3 to the standard output.
- Item 1 is Milk, but the price of Cheese is 2.35.

The correct answer is d.

# Answer Quiz 2

The first Quiz and this one are almost identical, except that this exercise declares the name and the price variables static.

- That means there is only one copy available for all the applications. It doesn't matter which object you use to access those variables.

- You can also use the class name to access those variables as follows.

```java
System.out.println(Item.name +", "+ Item.price);
```

The correct answer is b

# Answer Quiz 3

- Keep in mind that the ArrayList products is declared static.

- No matter which store object you add items to or remove them from, The result for both is the same because they have the exact copy of the list of products.

The correct answer is: a

## Answer Quiz 4

The average grade of all the students is the same as that of Layla because the last time, the getAverage() method was executed for the st3. That calculates the average is static. Therefore, only one copy of the method exists for all the objects.
The correct answer is a, b and c.

Output

```
Student name: Jack Average grade 8.0
Student name: Salma Average grade 8.0
Student name: Layla Average grade 8.0
```

## Answer Quiz 5

- Line 1 invokes the method getSum, which calculates the sum of 44 and -33.
- Line 2 prints the sum of the two numbers 44 and -33; the result is 11.
- Line 3 invokes the method getLargest, and the numbers 24 and 24 passed through it as parameters; therefore, it writes "equal" to the standard output.
- Line 4 invokes the method getLargest of 39 and 41, which prints 41 to the standard output.

The correct answer is a.

Output

```
11, equal, 41,
```

# 12. Exceptions

An exception is an abnormal condition that might occur during the execution of a program.
The exception objects in Java contain information about the errors. There are two types of Exceptions: **checked** and **unchecked** Exceptions.

The keywords handle exceptions: **try, catch, throw, throws,** and **finally.**

Exceptions might be caused by several reasons, for example,

* Entering letters in a field that is designed for calculating numbers.
* Trying to access the seventh element of an array of five elements
* Trying to access a file that doesn't exist.

All exceptions in Java are derived from the class Throwable. The following methods of the class Throwable are used to get information about the cause of the errors.

Diagram 1 shows the Exception class hierarchy in Java.

For further information about the class Throwable, see the online documentation of the Java standard API.

## Table 1: Method return types

| Method | Return type | Description |
| --- | --- | --- |
| printStackTrace() | void | Write the possible errors to the standard error-stream. |
| getMessage() | String | returns the message as a String. |

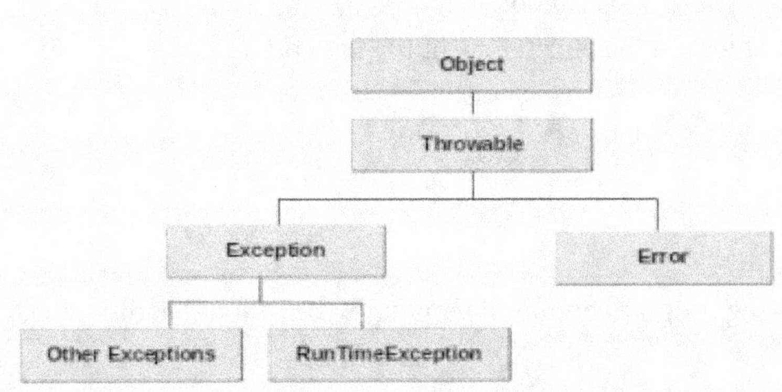


# RuntimeException (Unchecked)

The RuntimeException is unchecked, and the Java compiler does not enforce it. Programmers are free to ignore the RunTimeException. However, it is wise to handle these exceptions so that the users receive a message explaining the cause.

**Examples of unchecked exceptions:**

* ArithmeticException
* Divide-by-0: This exception occurs when a number is divided by zero.
* ClassCastException By illegal casting.
* IndexArrayOutOfBoundsException: If you try to access element 8 of an array of 7 elements, the IndexArrayOutOfBoundsException occurs.
* NullPointerException: The NullPointerException occurs when trying to access a member of an object reference before the object is created.

## Other Exceptions (Checked)

The checked exceptions cannot be ignored; programmers should handle them. Examples are the exceptions of the network connection, a file not found, etc.

## The Try-Catch Block

The following program divides a number by 0 without handling the exception.
Improve the program by handling the exception using try-catch.

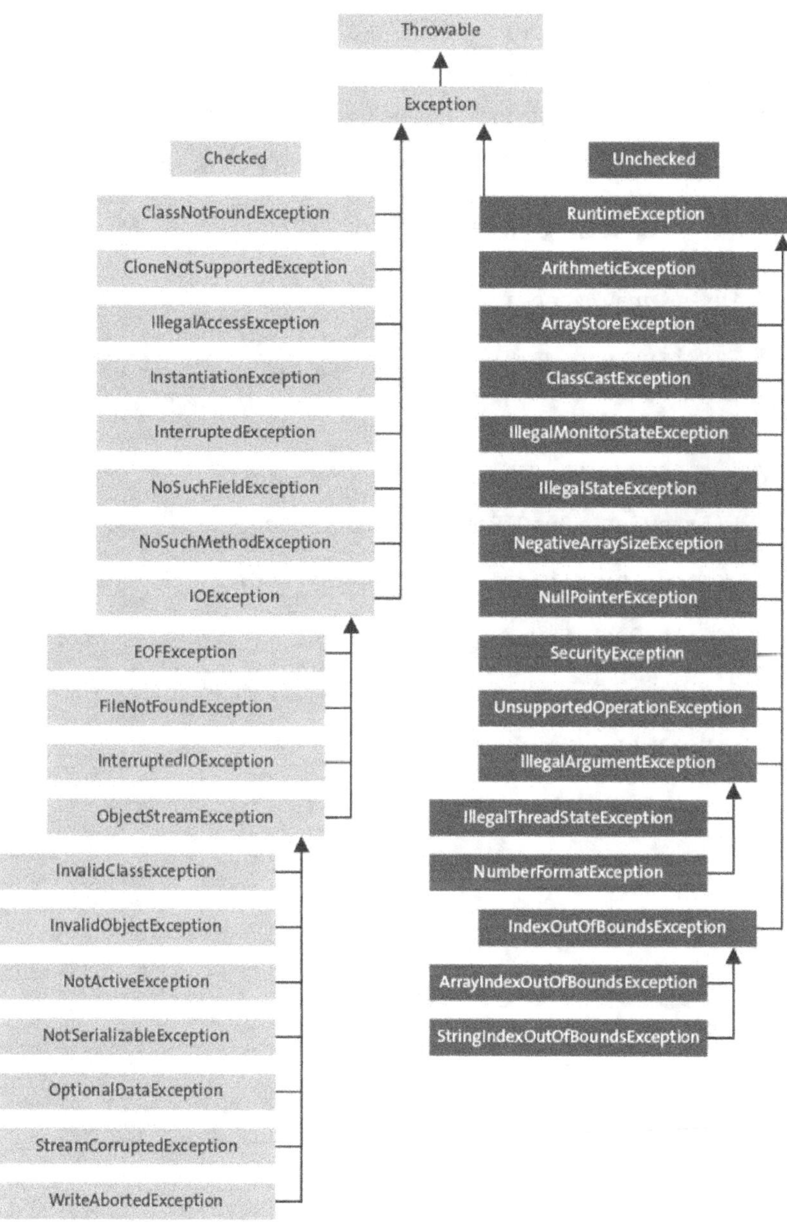


You can use as many catch-blocks under each other as necessary, but you need to remember the exceptions' order.

In the following example, the catch-block Exception is under the catch-block IndexOutOfBoundsException because the class Exception, in general, is higher than the class IndexOutOfBoundsException in the hierarchy of the exception classes. For the same reason, the catch block of IndexOutOfBoundsException is under the catch block of ArrayIndexOutOfBoundsException. See the above diagram.

## Example 1: Exception Hierarchy

```java
public class ArrayException
{
  public static void main(String[] args)
  {
    try
    {
      // A code which may cause an exception
    }
    catch(ArrayIndexOutOfBoundsException ae)
    {
      // catch the exception ArrayIndexOutOfBoundsException
    }
    catch(IndexOutOfBoundsException ae)
    {
      // catch the exception IndexOutOfBoundsException
    }
    catch(Exception e)
    {
      // catch all other possible exceptions
    }
  }
}
```

## Example 2: Divide by Zero

```java
public class Calculator
{
  public static void divide(int numerator, int denominator)
  {
    int result = numerator / denominator;
    System.out.println("Result: " + result);
  }
  public static void main(String[] args)
  {
    divide(20, 0);
  }
}
```

Output

```
Exception in thread "main" java.lang.ArithmeticException: /
by zero at Calculator.divide(Calculator.java:8)
    at Calculator.main(Calculator.java:13)
```

## *Example 2B: Divide by Zero Exception*

```java
public class Calculator
{
  public static void divide(int numerator, int denominator)
  {
    try
    {
      int result = numerator / denominator;
      System.out.println("Result: " + result);
    }
    catch(ArithmeticException e)
    {
      System.out.println("Error: " + e.getMessage());
    }
  }
  public static void main(String[] args)
  {
    divide(20, 0);
  }
}
```

Output

```
Error: / by zero
```

The program tries to divide an integer by an integer in the above code. If the denominator is zero, the catch exception is handled.

> **Notice**
>
> In the previous example, we didn't use the variable type double because by using double, the program says that the answer is infinity. The program's output is the standard message divided by zero, as shown below.

## *Example 2B2: Divide by Zero Exception*

```java
public class Calculator
{
  public static void divide(double numerator, double denominator)
  {
    double result = numerator / denominator;
    System.out.println("Result: " + result);
  }
  public static void main(String[] args)
  {
    divide(20, 0);
  }
}
```

Output

```
Result: Infinity
```

# The Finally-Block

The finally-block follows either the try or the catch block, and it is always executed whether exceptions occur. Finally, it is used, for example, to close a network connection or file. See the following example.

## *Example 2C: Division by Zero Finally*

```java
public class Calculator
{
  public static void divide(int numerator, int denominator)
  {
    try
    {
      int result = numerator / denominator;
      System.out.println("Result: " + result);
    }
    catch(ArithmeticException ae)
    {
      System.out.println("Error: " + ae.getMessage());
    }
    finally
    {
      System.out.println("The finally-block");
    }
```

```java
  }
  public static void main(String[] args)
  {
    divide(20, 0); //.... 1
  }
}
```

Output

```
Error: / by zero
The finally-block
```

# Example 2D: Division by Zero Finally

**Calculator.java**

```java
public class Calculator
{
  public static void divide(int numerator, int denominator)
  {
    try
    {
      int result = numerator / denominator;
      System.out.println("Result: " + result);
    }
    catch(ArithmeticException ae)
    {
      System.out.println(ae);
    }
    finally
    {
      System.out.println("The finally-block");
    }
  }
  public static void main(String[] args)
  {
    divide(20, 2); //.... 1
  }
}
```

Ouput

```
Result: 10
The finally-block
```

# The Keywords Throw and Throws

A Java code can throw an exception with the keywords throw and throws. You can catch these exceptions with a catch block. The keyword throws is used in the header of the methods, but the keyword throw is used in the body of the methods.

In the following program, a new object, IllegalArgumentException("Division by zero"), is thrown if the denominator is 0.

## *Example 2E: Division by Zero Throws, Throw*

**Calculator.java**

```java
public class Calculator
{
  public static double divide(double x, double n) throws
IllegalArgumentException
  {
    if(n == 0)
    {
      throw new IllegalArgumentException("Division by zero");
    }
    return x / n;
  }
  public static void main(String[] args)
  {
    double result = 0;

    try
    {
      result = divide(20, 0); //....1
    }
    catch(IllegalArgumentException iae)
    {
      System.out.println("\nException: " + iae.getMessage());
    }
    System.out.println("Result: " + result);
  }
}
```

Output

```
Exception: Division by zero
Result: 0.0
```

# Exaplanation

Line 1 invokes the method divide within the main method. The try-block tries to invoke the method with a zero denominator.

The method "divide" throws IllegalArgumentException when the denominator is zero. The word "Exception:" is printed, and the customized message "division by zero."

The double value of the result within the main method is zero. Therefore, it is also printed as 0.0.

## *Example 2F: Division by Zero Throw*

Change the statement of line 1 in the previous exercise from divide(20, 0) to divide(20, 2). What is the output of the program?

```
result = divide(20, 2); //....1
```

**Calculator.java**

```java
public class Calculator
{
  public static double divide(double x, double n) throws
IllegalArgumentException
  {
    if(n == 0)
    {
      throw new IllegalArgumentException("Division by zero");
    }
    return x / n;
  }
  public static void main(String[] args)
  {
    double result = 0;

    try
    {
      result = divide(20, 0); //....1
    }
    catch(IllegalArgumentException iae)
    {
      System.out.println("Exception: " + iae.getMessage());
    }
```

```java
        System.out.println("\nResult: " + result);
    }
}
```

Line 1 invokes the method divide within the main method. The try-block tries to invoke the method, which calculates the 20 divided by 2. The division is fine, and the try-block succeeds; therefore, the catch-block is ignored. The finally-block is always executed.

Output

```
Result: 10.0
```

# Customized Exception

## Create and Throw a Customized Exception Class

A customized exception class, MyException, is created in the following example. This class is a checked exception because it is a subclass of the class Exception.
If an exception occurs, you can show your customized text instead of the default one. The statement on line 1 divide(20, 0) divides 20 by zero. What is the output of the following code?

### *Example 3A: Customized Exception*

**MyException.java**

```java
public class MyException extends Exception
{
    public MyException(String message)
    {
        super(message);
    }
}
```

**Calculator.java**

```java
public class Calculator
{
```

```java
  public static double division(double numerator, double
                              denominator) throws MyException
  {
    if(denominator == 0)
    {
      throw new MyException("Division by zero");
    }
    return numerator / denominator;
  }
  public static void main(String[] args)
  {
    try
    {
      double result = division(20, 0); //...1
      System.out.println(result);
    }
    catch(MyException me)
    {
      System.out.println("\nException: " + me.getMessage());
    }
  }
}
```

# Explanation 3A

The statement on line 1 divide (20, 0) invokes the method divide, which
throws a customized exception with a customized message. The exception
MyException is used within the main method.
The try-block fails to calculate the result; therefore, the following
customized message is printed to the standard output.

Output

```
Exception: Division by zero
```

## *Example 3B:*

Change the statement on line 1 to divide(20, 2) and rerun the program. What
is the output of the program?

```java
double result = division(20, 2); //...1
System.out.println(result);
```

# Explanation 3B

In this case, the try-block succeeds in calculating 20 divided by 2; therefore, 10.0 is printed to the standard output.

Output

```
10.0
```

# Error Class

The Error class is a subclass of the class Throwable. Errors can occur at runtime, and programmers usually do not have control over them. Examples are StackOverflowError, OutOfMemoryError, and UnknowError.

## *Quiz 1: Unchecked exception*

The following examples use the method parseInt to change a $ sign to an integer.

What happens when the following program is compiled and run?

**MyList.java**

```java
public class MyText
{
  public void method()
  {
    try
    {
      System.out.print("N");
      Integer.parseInt("$4");
      System.out.print("T");
    }
    catch(NumberFormatException e)
    {
      System.out.print("W");
    }
  }
  public static void main(String[] args)
  {
    MyText mt = new MyText();
    mt.method();
  }
}
```

Select the correct answer:

a. This program writes "N$4T" to the standard output.

b. This program writes "N" to the standard output.

c. This program writes "NW" to the standard output.

d. This program writes "W" to the standard output.

e. This program writes nothing to the standard output.

## Quiz 2: The Finally-Block

What happens when the following program is compiled and run?

**MyList.java**

```java
public class MyList
{
  public void method()
  {
    try
    {
      int[] listNr = new int[7];
      int L = listNr[9]; //......1
      System.out.print(L);
    }
    catch(ArithmeticException e)
    {
      System.out.print("V");
    }
    catch(ArrayIndexOutOfBoundsException e)
    {
      System.out.print("W");
    }
    finally
    {
      System.out.print("N");
    }
  }
  public static void main(String[] args)
  {
    MyList ml = new MyList();
    ml.method();
  }
}
```

Select the correct answer:

a. This program writes "LN" to the standard output.

b. This program writes "WN" to the standard output.

c. This program writes "0WN" to the standard output.

d. This program writes "VN" to the standard output.

e. This program writes nothing to the standard output.

## *Quiz 2B: The Finally-Block*

What is the output of the previous exercise if you change the statement on line 1 to the following?

```java
int L = listNr[5]; //.....1
```

**MyList.java**

```java
public class MyList
{
  public void method()
  {
    try
    {
      int[] listNr = new int[7];
      int L = listNr[5]; //.....1
      System.out.print(L);
    }
    catch(ArithmeticException e)
    {
      System.out.print("V");
    }
    catch(ArrayIndexOutOfBoundsException e)
    {
      System.out.print("W");
    }
    finally
    {
      System.out.print("N");
    }
  }
  public static void main(String[] args)
  {
    MyList ml = new MyList();
    ml.method();
  }
}
```

Select the correct answer:

a. This program writes "LN" to the standard output.

b. This program writes "LWN" to the standard output.

c. This program writes "0WN" to the standard output.

d. This program writes "0N" to the standard output.

e. This program writes nothing to the standard output.

## Quiz 3: Unchecked Exception & Finally

What happens when the following program is compiled and run?

**MyText.java**

```java
public class MyText
{
  String str; //........................1
  public void method()
  {
    try
    {
      String R = str.substring(2, 3); //..2
      System.out.print(R);
    }
    catch(NullPointerException e)
    {
      System.out.print("S");
    }
    catch(Exception e)
    {
      System.out.print("T");
    }
    finally
    {
      System.out.print("W");
    }
  }
  public static void main(String[] args)
  {
    MyText mt = new MyText();
    mt.method();
  }
}
```

Select the correct answer:

a. This program writes "SW" to the standard output.

b. This program writes "RTW" to the standard output.

c. This program writes "TW" to the standard output.

d. This program writes "W" to the standard output.

e. This program writes "RW" to the standard output.

## Quiz 3B: Unchecked Exception Finally

What is the output of the previous code if you change the statement on line 1 to the following?

```
String str = "DAVID"; //.....1
```

**MyText.java**

```java
public class MyText
{
   String str = "DAVID"; //................1

   public void method()
   {
     try
     {
       String R = str.substring(2, 3); //..2
       System.out.print(R);
     }
     catch(NullPointerException e)
     {
       System.out.print("S");
     }
     catch(Exception e)
     {
       System.out.print("T");
     }
     finally
     {
       System.out.print("W");
     }
   }
   public static void main(String[] args)
   {
     MyText mt = new MyText();
     mt.method();
   }
}
```

Select the correct answer:

a. This program writes "SW" to the standard output.

b. This program writes "VW" to the standard output.

c. This program writes "TW" to the standard output.

d. This program writes "W" to the standard output.

e. This program writes "AVW" to the standard output.

## Quiz 3C: Uncehcked Exception Finally

What is the output of the previous code if you change the statement on line 1 to the following?

```
String str = "DJ"; // ...............1
```

**MyText.java**

```
public class MyTexl
{
  String str = "DJ"; // ..................1

  public void method()
  {
    try
    {
      String R = str.substring(2, 3); //..2
      System.out.print(R);
    }
    catch(NullPointerException e)
    {
      System.out.print("S");
    }
    catch(Exception e)
    {
      System.out.print("T");
    }
    finally
    {
      System.out.print("W");
    }
  }
  public static void main(String[] args)
  {
```

```java
    MyText mt = new MyText();
    mt.method();
  }
}
```

Select the correct answer:

a. This program writes "SW" to the standard output.

b. This program writes "VW" to the standard output.

c. This program writes "TW" to the standard output.

d. This program writes "W" to the standard output.

e. This program writes "JW" to the standard output.

## Quiz 3D: Unchecked Exception Finally

What is the output of the program If we change the previous code to the following?

```java
public class MyText
{
  String str = "DJ"; // .....1
  public void method()
  {
    try
    {
      String R = str.substring(2, 3); //..2
      System.out.print(R);
    }
    catch(NullPointerException e)
    {
      System.out.print("S");
    }
    catch(StringIndexOutOfBoundsException siob)
    {
      System.out.print("H");
    }
    catch(Exception e)
    {
      System.out.print("T");
    }
    finally
    {
      System.out.print("W");
    }
  }
  public static void main(String[] args)
```

```
  {
    MyText mt = new MyText();
    mt.method();
  }
}
```

Select the correct answer:

a. This program writes "SW" to the standard output.

b. This program writes "HW" to the standard output.

c. This program writes "TW" to the standard output.

d. This program writes "W" to the standard output.

e. This program writes nothing to the standard output.

## Quiz 4: Which Exception Is Handled?

What happens when the following program is compiled and run?

```java
public class MyClass
{
  StringBuffer sb;
  int Z;

  public void myMethod()
  {
    try
    {
      int G = 5 / Z; //.....1
      sb.append("S"); //....2
    }
    catch(NullPointerException e)
    {
      System.out.print("N");
    }
    catch(ArithmeticException ae)
    {
      System.out.print("A");
    }
    catch(Exception e)
    {
      System.out.print("T");
    }
  }
  public static void main(String[] args)
```

```
    {
      MyClass mc = new MyClass();
      mc.myMethod();
    }
}
```

Select the correct answer:

a. This code writes N to the standard output.

b. This code writes AN to the standard output.

c. This code writes A to the standard output.

d. This code writes NA to the standard output.

e. This code writes nothing to the standard output.

## Quiz 4B: Which Exception?

What happens when we change the positions of line 1 and line 2 in the previous code? Assuming that the code is compiled and run.

```
public class MyClass
{
  StringBuffer sb;
  int Z;

  public void myMethod()
  {
    try
    {
      sb.append("S"); //....2
      int G = 5 / Z; //.....1
    }
    catch(NullPointerException e)
    {
      System.out.print("N");
    }
    catch(ArithmeticException ae)
    {
      System.out.print("A");
    }
    catch(Exception e)
    {
      System.out.print("T");
    }
```

```
    }
  public static void main(String[] args)
  {
    MyClass mc = new MyClass();
    mc.myMethod();
  }
}
```

Select the correct answer:

a. This code writes N to the standard output.

b. This code writes AN to the standard output.

c. This code writes A to the standard output.

d. This code writes NA to the standard output.

e. This code writes nothing to the standard output.

## Quiz 5: Throw New Exception

What happens when the following program is compiled and run?

```
public class MyClass
{
  static String text = "";

  static void calculate(int x, int y)
  {
    text += "G";

    if(y == 0)
    {
      throw new ArithmeticException(); //..1
    }
    int z = x / y;
    text += "H";
  }
  public static void main(String[] args)
  {
    try
    {
      text += "I";
      calculate(10, 0);
      text += "K";
    }
    catch(ArithmeticException ae)
    {
      text += "L";
```

```
      }
      catch(NullPointerException ne)
      {
        text += "M";
      }
      System.out.println(text);
  }
}
```

Select the correct answer:

a. This code writes GHL to the standard output.

b. This code writes IGM to the standard output.

c. This code writes IGL to the standard output.

d. This code writes GHIK to the standard output.

e. This code writes GLM to the standard output.

## Quiz 5B: Throw New Exception

What is the output of the previous code if the statement on line 1 is changed to throw **NullPointerException** instead of ArithmeticException, as shown below?

```
public class MyClass
{
  static String text = "";
  static void calculate(int x, int y)
  {
    text += "G";

    if(y == 0)
    {
      throw new NullPointerException();//..1
    }
    int z = x / y;
    text += "H";
  }
  public static void main(String[] args)
  {
    try
    {
      text += "I";
      calculate(10, 0);
      text += "K";
    }
    catch(ArithmeticException ae)
```

```
      {
        text += "L";
      }
      catch(NullPointerException ne)
      {
        text += "M";
      }
      System.out.println(text);
    }
}
```

Select the correct answer:

a. This code writes GHL to the standard output.

b. This code writes IGM to the standard output.

c. This code writes IGL to the standard output.

d. This code writes GHIK to the standard output.

e. This code writes GLM to the standard output.

## *Quiz 6: Keyword Throw*

What happens when the following program is compiled and run?

```java
public class MyClass
{
  public static void myMethod(String str)
  {
    if(str == null)
    {
      throw new NullPointerException();
    }
    else
    {
      throw new RuntimeException();
    }
  }
  public static void main(String[] args)
  {
    try
    {
      System.out.print("G");
      myMethod("");
    }
    catch(NullPointerException e)
    {
```

```java
    System.out.print("H");
  }
  catch(Exception e)
  {
    System.out.print("K");
  }
  finally
  {
    System.out.print("N");
  }
 }
}
```

Select the correct answer:

a. This code writes G to the standard output.

b. This code writes GH to the standard output.

c. This code writes GKN to the standard output.

d. This code writes GHN to the standard output.

e. This code writes GK to the standard output.

## Exercise 1 Library Application

Write a program that allows users to enter a unique book ID of books in a library.

- If the book exists in the system, the program writes the title of the book.
- If the user enters an ID of a book that doesn't exist, the program informs the user that the book doesn't exist.
- If the user mistakenly enters a letter or a sign, the program also notifies the user to enter a number.

Here are some possible outputs, depending on the user input.

Output 1

```
Please enter the book id: 7
Book 7 is: Database Design and SQL
```

Output 2

```
Please enter the book id: 44
Book: 44 is not found.
```

Output 3

```
Please enter the book id: x
The input is not a number.
```

## Answers to the Quizzes and the Exercises

# Answer Quiz 1

- The statement "System.out.print("N");" in the try block prints "N" to the standard output.
- The statement "Integer.parseInt("$4");" tries to parse the string argument, which contains a dollar sign as an integer.
- The $ sign is not an integer; therefore, the program executes the catch block NumberFormatException.
- The statement "System.out.print("W");" prints "W" to the standard output.

The correct answer is c.

# Answer Quiz 2

- The statement "int N = listNr[9];" on line 1 tries to access the ninth element of the array listNr, which doesn't exist.
- The exception ArithmeticException has nothing to do with the index of the array's elements; therefore, it will be ignored.
- The exception ArrayIndexOutOfBoundsException occurs, and the statement System.out.print("W"), prints "W" to the standard output.

- The finally-block is always executed.
- The statement System.out.print("N"), prints "N" to the standard output.  The code prints WN to the standard output.

The correct answer is b.

# Answer Quiz 2B

- The try-block prints the element with index 5 of the array listNr, which has seven elements.
- The integer elements of the array are not initialized; therefore, they have the zero standard int value in Java.
- The try-block doesn't cause any exceptions; therefore, the exception blocks are ignored.
- The finally block is always executed and it writes "N" to the standard output. The output of the code is 0N.

The correct answer is d.

# Answer Quiz 3

- The String str refers to an object that is not created; therefore, it is "null."
- By trying to access a substring of str, a NullPointerException occurs.
- The statement System.out.print("S"), prints the letter "S" to the standard output.
- The final block is always executed. The statement System.out.print("W"), prints the letter "W" to the standard output.

The correct answer is a.

# Answer Quiz 3B

- The string on line 1 is not null anymore but an object.

- The statement on line 2 returns the substring of 2, 3.
- Index 2 of DAVID starting with zero is "V." The substring of index three is not included.
- Therefore, the letter V is printed, and the letter W is the finally-block. The output is VW.

The correct answer is b.

# Answer Quiz 3C

- The statement str. substring(2, 3) causes an exception because the substring of 2 and three of the string "DJ" doesn't exist.
- Therefore, the exception block is executed, and the program prints TW to the standard output.

The correct answer is c.

# Answer Quiz 3D

- In this case, the general exception block is ignored because the code contains the exception block "StringIndexOutOfBoundsException," which is a more specific exception for the string. The output of the code is HW.

The correct answer is b.

# Answer Quiz 4

- The two statements on lines 1 and 2 of the try-block cause exceptions, but statement 1 is first executed.
- Therefore, it causes an ArithmetcException; therefore, its block is executed.
- The statement System.out.print("A"); writes A to the standard output.

The correct answer is c.

# Answer Quiz 4B

- This time, the statement "sb.append("S"); //...2" causes the exception.
- Since the StringBuffer sb is a reference to an object that still needs to be created.
- The NullPointerException-block is executed, and the code writes N to the standard output.

The correct answer is a.

# Answer Quiz 5

- The main method is executed, and it starts with the try-block. First statement text += I adds the letter I to the text.
- The statement calculate(10, 0) calls the method calculate.
- The statement text += "G" within the method calculation adds the letter G to the string text.
- The statement if(y == 0) returns true, and the exception ArithmeticException is thrown.
- The catch block of the exception, ArithmeticException, is caught.
- The statement text += "L" adds the letter L to the String text.

The correct answer is c.

# Answer Quiz 5B

- In this example, the code still writes the "IG," but this time, the block NullPointerException is invoked and prints IGM to the standard output.

The correct answer is b.

# Answer Quiz 6

- The statement System.out.print("G"); within the try-block, writes G to the standard output

- The method myMethod("") is invoked.

- If the statement if(str == null) returns true, the exception NullPointerException is handled; otherwise, a RuntimeException.

- The method myMethod("") parameter is not equal to null. Therefore, the RuntimeException is thrown.

- The catch block Exception is higher in the exception class hierarchy than the RuntimeException, which is why it is caught.

- See the diagram of the exception for the exception class hierarchy.

- The statement System.out.print("K"); writes the letter K to the standard output.

- The finally-block is always executed; therefore, the letter N is also written to the standard output.

The correct answer is c.

# Answer Exercise 1

**Book.java**

```java
public class Book
{
  private int id;
  private String title;

  Book(int id, String title)
  {
    this.id = id;
    this.title = title;
  }
  public int getId()
  {
    return id;
  }
  public void setId(int id)
  {
    this.id = id;
  }
  public String getTitle()
  {
    return title;
  }
  public void setTitle(String title)
```

```java
  {
    this.title = title;
  }
}
```

## Library.java

```java
import java.util.ArrayList;
import java.util.List;

public class Library
{
  private List<Book> books;

  public Library()
  {
    this.books = new ArrayList<>();
    populateList();
  }
  private void addBook(int id, String title)
  {
    books.add(new Book(id, title));
  }
  private void populateList()
  {
    addBook(1, "Learn Java");
    addBook(2, "Java Advanced");
    addBook(3, "Learn Python");
    addBook(4, "Advanced C++");
    addBook(5, "PHP for Beginners");
    addBook(6, "Learn HTML");
    addBook(7, "Database Design and SQL");
    addBook(8, "UML");
    addBook(9, "Object Oriented Programming");
    addBook(10, "Linux Operating System");
  }
  public Book getBookById(int id) throws MyException
  {
    for (Book book : books)
    {
      if(book.getId() == id)
      {
        System.out.println("Book " + id + " is: "+book.getTitle());
        return book;
      }
    }
    throw new MyException("Book: " + id + " is not found.");
  }
}
```

## MainApp.java

```java
import java.util.InputMismatchException;
import java.util.Scanner;

public class MainApp
{
  public static void main(String args[])
  {
    try (Scanner input = new Scanner(System.in))
    {
      System.out.print("\nPlease enter the book id: ");
      int id = input.nextInt();
      Library lb = new Library();

      try
      {
        lb.getBookById(id);
      }
      catch(MyException me)
      {
        System.out.println(me.getMessage());
      }
    }
    catch(InputMismatchException e)
    {
      System.out.println("The input is not a number.");
    }
  }
}
```

## MyException.java

```java
public class MyException extends Exception
{
  public MyException()
  {
    super();
  }
  public MyException(String message)
  {
    super(message);
  }
  public MyException(Throwable cause)
  {
    super(cause);
  }
  public MyException(String message, Throwable cause)
  {
    super(message, cause);
  }
}
```

# 13. Java Memory Management

## Stack and heap memory

The memory in Java is divided into two types: the stack and the heap.
The stack memory is used for local primitive variables such as int double
and object references. On the other hand, objects such as String and others
created by programmers are stored on the heap.

## The Life Cycle of Objects

The lifetime of an object In Java starts from the moment the object is
created to the moment it is destroyed.
The life cycle of objects concerns their creation and their existence in the
memory until they are finally destroyed. Understanding this process helps
developers to create objects at the right moment and understand the life
process of the objects in the memory.

Here below are the steps of the life cycle of objects.

1. The process starts with saving the bytecode in a class file with the
   name of the class and the extension ".class."
2. In the next step, the class is loaded into the memory.
3. The following step looks for the initialized static members: fields,
   methods, or blocks. Remember that static members belong to the
   class, and only one copy of them is shared by all the class objects.
4. A class is initialized when an object is created from it, or a static
   class member is accessed.
5. Once an object is created, memory is allocated on the heap, but its
   reference would be stored on the stack, as explained before.
6. Then, the class's constructor is called when the object is created. The
   statements inside the constructor are executed, and the object is
   initialized.

7. The object remains in the memory and provides access to its public members to other parts of the program whenever they need it.

8. When an object has no references pointing to it, it will be destroyed and removed from the memory.

## Quiz 1: Initializer

In the following code, the "main" method body is empty. What happens if the code is compiled and run? What is your explanation for the output?

**Bird.java**

```java
public class Bird
{
  int age1 = getAge(2);

  Bird()
  {
    int age2 = getAge(4);
  }
  static
  {
    System.out.print(getAge(6));
  }

  static int age4 = getAge(8);
  int age5 = getAge(20);

  public static int getAge(int age)
  {
    System.out.print(age);
    return age;
  }
  public static void main(String[] args)
  {
  }
}
```

Select the correct answer.

a. This code writes "668" to the standard output.

b. This code writes "68" to the standard output.

c. This code writes "6" to the standard output.

d. This code writes "8" to the standard output.

e. This code writes "null" to the standard output.

f. This code writes nothing to the standard output.

## Quiz 1B: Initializer

We use the code of the previous example, but this time, we create an object
of Bird within the main method.

```java
public class Bird
{
  int age1 = getAge(2);

  Bird()
  {
    int age2 = getAge(4);
  }
  static
  {
    int age3 = getAge(6);
  }

  static int age4 = getAge(8);
  int age5 = getAge(9);

  public static int getAge(int age)
  {
    System.out.print(age);
    return age;
  }
  public static void main(String[] args)
  {
    Bird bird = new Bird();
  }
}
```

Select the correct answer.

a. This code writes "668" to the standard output.

b. This code writes "68" to the standard output.

c. This code writes "684" to the standard output.

d. This code writes "68294" to the standard output.

e. This code writes "null" to the standard output.

f. This code writes nothing to the standard output.

## *Exercise 1: Object Initialization*

The following code works fine, but the issue is that the customer class creates an account object when it is unnecessary. The output of the code shows that two different account objects are instantiated.
Change the code to fix that issue.

**Account.java**

```java
public class Account
{
   private String username;
   private String password;
}
```

**Customer.java**

```java
public class Customer
{
  Account account = new Account();

  public Customer(Account account)
  {
    System.out.println("Account attribute: " + this.account);
    System.out.println("Account argument:  " + account);
    this.account = account;
  }
}
```

**MainApp.java**

```java
public class MainApp
{
   public static void main(String[] args) {
      Account account = new Account();
      Customer customer = new Customer(account);
   }
}
```

Output

```
Account attribute: Account@251a69d7
Account argument:  Account@6b95977
```

# Garbage Collection

Java garbage collection is an automatic process that manages the program's memory. After compiling a Java program, the bytecode can be run on a Java Virtual Machine (JVM). Java objects are created on the heap, part of the program's memory. When no references point to an object, the object becomes unnecessary. Therefore, the garbage collector removes the unused objects to free up memory.

As a programmer, you don't need to determine which objects should be garbage collected because that happens automatically.

## Objects are eligible for garbage collection?

1. When no references point to an object, it is eligible for garbage collection.
2. It is not possible to invoke the garbage collector directly, but programmers can suggest the JVM to perform garbage collection by calling System.gc().

### *Quiz 2: Eligible for Garbage Collection*

Which is the earliest line in the following code, after which object "employee" created on line 1 can be garbage collected? Assuming no compile optimization is done. Try to support your answer by clarifying for someone who doesn't understand your answer.

**Employee.java**

```java
public class Employee
{
  String name = "Emma";

  public static void main(String args[])
```

```java
  {
    Employee emp = new Employee();
    emp.createEmployee();
  }
  void createEmployee()
  {
    Employee employee = new Employee(); //.......line 1
    Employee[] employees = new Employee[7]; //..line 2
    employees[5] = employee; //.................line 3
    employee = null; //.........................line 4
  }
}
```

Select the correct answer.

a. After line 1.

b. After line 2.

c. After line 3.

d. After line 4.

e. It is impossible to determine that.

## *Quiz 3: Garbage collection*

Which is the earliest line in the MainApp class code, after which the object "computer" created on line 1 is eligible for garbage collection? Assuming no compile optimization is done. Prove the correctness of your answer if someone needs help understanding it.

**Computer.java**

```java
public class Computer
{
  String brand = "DELL";
}
```

**MainApp.java**

```java
public class MainApp
{
  private Computer computer;

  void setComputer(Computer computer)
  {
    this.computer = computer;
  }
```

```java
public static void main(String[] args)
{
   Computer computer = new Computer(); //..1
   MainApp ma = new MainApp();   //.........2
   ma.setComputer(computer); //............3
   computer = new Computer(); //...........4
   computer = null; //.....................5
   ma = new MainApp(); //..................6
}
}
```

Select the correct answer.

a. After line 1.

b. After line 2.

c. After line 3.

d. After line 4.

e. After line 5.

f. After line 6.

g. It is impossible to determine that.

## Memory in Java

Programmers must understand the process of running a piece of code and how the memory manages that.
That will also clarify the process of garbage collection. The memory has two main sections: The stack and the heap.

The stack holds the primitive variables and the references to the objects while the objects are created on the heap. The stack and the heap memories work together to manage the variables, object references, and objects. When our code is run, it requires access to the memory.

## The Stack memory

We start with the stack memory first and show how it works.
To understand the process, I have written a piece of code and clarified the process with straightforward illustrations, as shown below.

We use this simple code and look at the execution step by step and the state of the stack memory by each line. Through this simple code, we understand how variable scope works and how variables declared in one method are only visible in that method. Through this code, we try to understand how variables passed through a process are managed in the memory.

## *Example 1: Stack Memory*

What happens on the stack when you run the following code?

**Item.java**

```java
public class Item
{
  public static void main(String[] args) //.........1
  {
    double initialPrice = 50; //....................2
    initialPrice = getPrice(initialPrice); //......6
  }
  public static double getPrice(double price) //...3
  {
    double discount = price * 0.20; //.............4
    double lastPrice = price - discount;
    return lastPrice; //...........................5
  }
}
```

# Explanation

What happens in the memory step by step

- The execution starts with the main method. An array of strings is passed as a parameter through the main method. That will occupy the top of the stock.

- The next step is the double-type variable initialPrice that gets pushed to the top of the stack.

- The following line that would be reached is the method getPrice through which the copy of the variable initialPrice is passed called price. As the execution enters the getPrice method, a new variable, price, is added to the stack. By entering the getPrice method, the main method is pushed down the stack, and its variables would be out of scope for the body lines of execution of the getPrice method.

- In the body of the method getPrice, two local variables are declared, which calculates the variable's discount and the last price. The execution reaches the variable discount and calculates the discount. The variable discount would be added to the top of the stack.

- At last, the method returns the value of the variable lastPrice. When the method returns the value, all the data created on the stack for that method is pulled out.

- The execution of the method getPrice is finished, and it goes back to the main method to reassign the value of the variable lastPrice with the returned value of the method.

## Stack

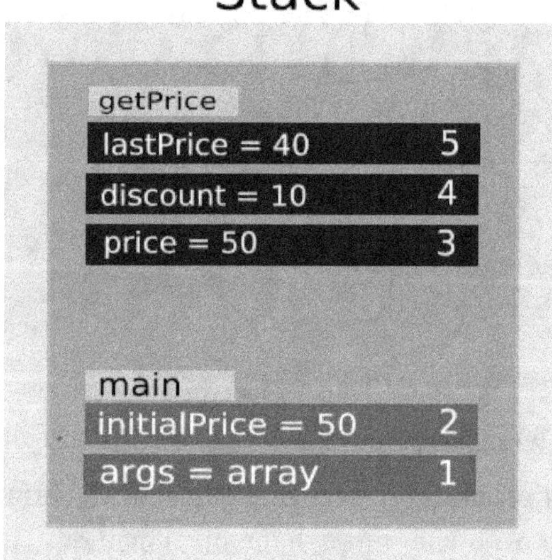


After those steps, the final closing bracket is reached, and at that point, the stack will be empty, and all the variables will be destroyed.

In Java, local variables are created on the stack, and they are automatically removed when the execution reaches the final closing bracket of the block. The stock memory will be empty after reaching the final closing brackets of the blocks.

# Stack

## The Heap memory

The second memory area, the heap, allows for storing data with a longer
lifetime than a single code block, such as methods.
The heap is a significant area for storing objects, and it is essential to
understand that all the objects are stored on the heap while the stack is used
to store local primitive variables such as int and double. Objects such as
strings, arrays, and others are created on the heap, but their references are
stored on the stack.

### *Example 2: Heap Memory*

**MainApp.java**

```java
import java.util.ArrayList;
import java.util.List;

public class MainApp
{
```

```java
public static void main(String[] args)
{
  List<String> countries = new ArrayList<String>(); //...1
  countries.add("Germany"); //............................2
  countries.add("Canada"); //.............................3
  countries.add("Japan"); //..............................4

  String myCountry = countries.get(0);
}
}
```

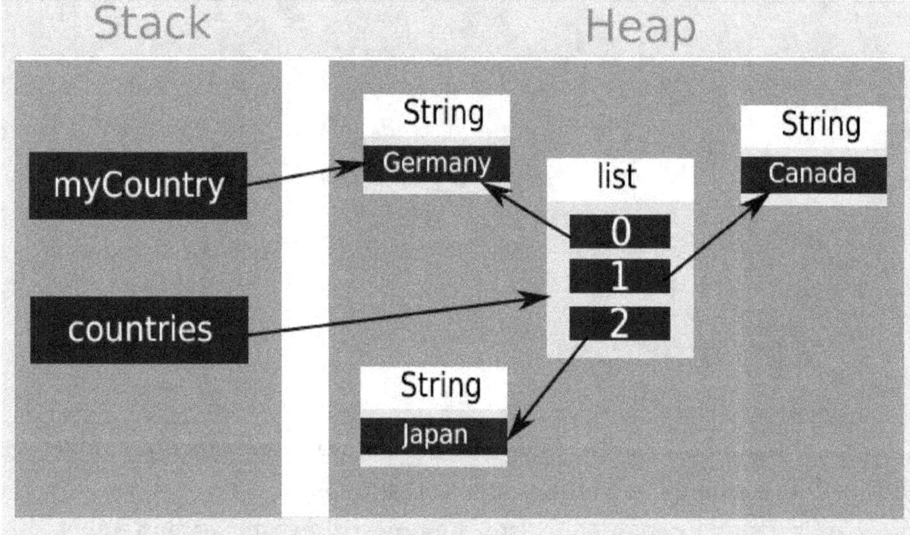


To simplify the diagram, we keep the parameter args array of the main method outside the diagram. The heap area, in reality, is much larger than the stack area because it holds all the objects of the application.

Let's see what the execution of the code looks like in the memory.

The first line of code will create the list object of the countries. Using the new keyword will make room on the heap for the list object. The reference will be on the stack called countries.

- The following line adds a string object country Germany to the list. Java will create the string object on the heap with the value

Germany, which will be interesting because nothing will be created on the stack for that list element. There is no local variable reference to the element Germany. The reference is only in the list object; we cannot call it directly. The access will be through the list object's index.

- As we go on with the code, other strings are created the same way, repeating the process. Remember that the diagram is only to clarify the process for programmers, but the places of the objects are not the same as in the memory. We can access these element objects through their references in the heap. Accessing the elements is by using their index within the list. The way to access the third country on the list is:

```java
String myCountry = countries.get(0);
```

## Memory and the final references

In Java, the final keyword is often used to prevent unintentional value changes. In the following example, the final reference myCar points to the object Car on the heap.

The brand of the car points to the value of Cadillac on the heap, as shown in the image below. The following code produced an error because it tries to reassign a new value to a final reference, myCar.

### *Example 3A: Memory and Final References*

Reassigning the final field, myCar, in the class MainApp causes an error, because myCar is final.

**Car.java**

```java
public class Car
{
  private String brand;

  public Car(String brand)
  {
```

```java
    this.brand = brand;
  }
  public String getBrand()
  {
    return brand;
  }
  public void setBrand(String brand)
  {
    this.brand = brand;
  }
}
```

## MainApp.java

```java
public class MainApp
{
  public static void main(String[] args)
  {
    final Car myCar = new Car("Cadillac");
    // reassign a new value to the final myChar
    myCar = new Car("BMW");
    System.out.println("Brand: " + myCar.getBrand());
    myCar.setBrand("BMW");
    System.out.println("Brand: " + myCar.getBrand());
  }
}
```

Let's look at the following final reference and see whether we can get around and change the final value.

## *Example 3B: Memory and Final References*

What happens in the memory when you run a code like the following?

## Car.java

```java
public class Car
{
  private String brand;

  public Car(String brand)
  {
    this.brand = brand;
  }
  public String getBrand()
  {
    return brand;
```

```
  }
  public void setBrand(String brand)
  {
    this.brand = brand;
  }
}
```

## MainApp.java

```
public class MainApp
{
  public static void main(String[] args)
  {
    final Car myCar = new Car("Cadillac");
    System.out.println("Brand: " + myCar.getBrand());

    myCar.setBrand("BMW");
    System.out.println("Brand: " + myCar.getBrand());
  }
}
```

# Explanation

The final reference, myCar, points to the car object on the heap; however,
the attribute brand points to the String object Cadillac on the heap.

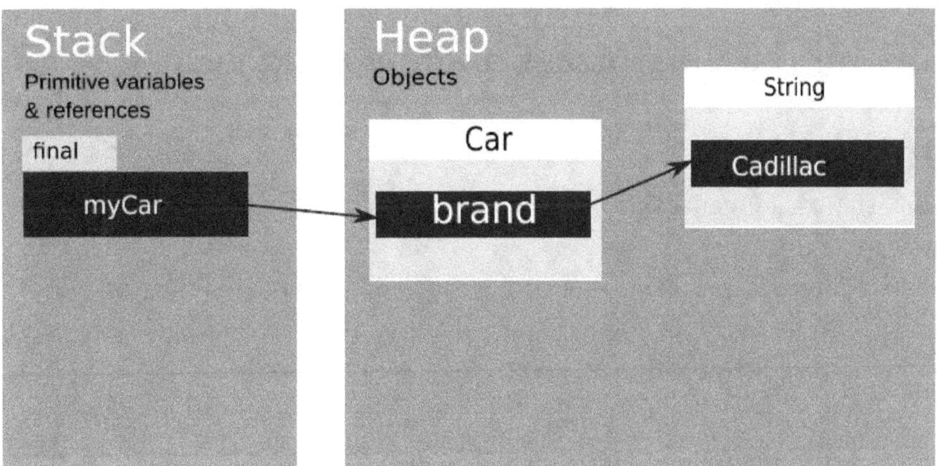

Pointing the final reference myCar to another Car object on the heap is impossible. However, as shown below, the brand attribute can point to another String object, BMW, on the heap.

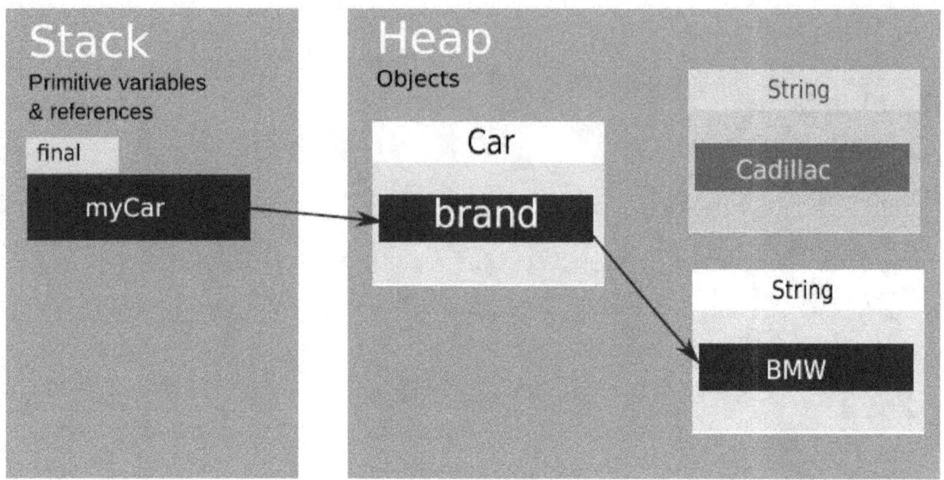


Based on the above explanation, the code output is as follows.

```
Brand: Cadillac
Brand: BMW
```

## Answers to the Quizzes and the Exercises

# Answer Quiz 1

First, static statements and static blocks are executed in the order in which they are defined.

- There are no statements within the main method, but the program still writes "668" to the standard output because the static statements and static blocks are called independent objects.
- The first static block in the code invokes the method getAge(6) and prints the return number, which is also 6.
- The return value 6 is also printed in the static block. Therefore, the number 6 is printed twice.
- Next, the statement getAge(8) is invoked, which prints 8 to the standard output.

The correct answer is a.

## Answer Quiz 1B

First, static statements and static blocks are executed in the order in which they are defined. Next, instance initializer statements and blocks are executed in the order they are defined. Finally, the constructor is executed.

- Based on the above explanation, the first static block invokes the method getAge(6), which prints the number 6 to the standard output.
- The second static field invokes the method getAge(8), which prints 8.
- The statement within the main method creates an object bird.
- By creating a bird object, the attribute ag1 invokes the method getAge(2) and prints 2.
- The following instance initializer invokes the method getAge(9) prints 9.
- At last, the constructor is called, which invokes the method getAge(4) and prints 4.
- The output is 68294.

The correct answer is d.

## Answer Quiz 2

It is impossible to determine after which line the object employee is eligible for garbage collection because a reference to the object employee remains even after line 4.

- To prove that, we use checkpoints after the creation of the object and at the end of the code.
- The reference employee[0] points to the object employee on line 3, and that reference remains till the end of the method.
- Two checking points are placed under line 1, where the object is created, and the second one under line 4, where the object employee is pointed to null.

- The element with index 5 of the array employees[5] still points to the same object.

The correct answer is e.

**Employee.java**

```java
public class Employee
{
  String name = "Emma";

  public static void main(String args[])
  {
    Employee emp = new Employee();
    emp.createEmployee();
  }
  void createEmployee()
  {
    Employee employee = new Employee();//..........line 1
    System.out.println(employee.name);//...........checkpoint 1
    Employee[] employees = new Employee[7];//..... line 2
    employees[5] = employee; //....................line 3
    employee = null; //...........................line 4
    System.out.println(employees[5].name); //......checkpoint 2
  }
}
```

The following is written to the standard if the above code is compiled and run.

output

```
Emma
Emma
```

# Answer Quiz 3

The first line creates a computer object with the reference "computer."

- On line 2, the object ma is created from the class MainApp, which contains a computer attribute.
- On line 3, the object computer is set to the attribute computer of the object ma.

- On line 4, the object created on line 1 points to a new object, but the object ma. The computer still points to the object computer on the first line.
- On line 5, the object created on line 1 points to null, but the attribute computer in the ma object still points to the computer designed on line 1.
- On line 6, ma is pointed to a new object, MainApp, which results in its attribute being set to null.
- The correct answer is after the line 6.

This explanation could be proven by adding checkpoints after each line to see whether the object changes, as shown in the code below.

The correct answer is f.

## Computer.java

```java
public class Computer
{
  String brand = "DELL";
}
```

## MainApp.java

```java
public class MainApp
{
  private Computer computer;

  void setComputer(Computer computer)
  {
    this.computer = computer;
  }
  public static void main(String[] args)
  {
    System.out.println("-----line 1-----");
    Computer computer = new Computer(); //...1
    System.out.println("computer: " + computer.brand);
    System.out.println("-----line 2-----");
    MainApp ma = new MainApp(); //............2
    System.out.println("computer: " + computer.brand);
    System.out.println("ma.computer: " + ma.computer);
    System.out.println("-----line 3-----");
    ma.setComputer(computer); //.............3
```

```java
        System.out.println("computer: " + computer);
        System.out.println("ma.computer: " + ma.computer);
        System.out.println("-----line 4-----");
        computer = new Computer(); //............4
        System.out.println("computer: " + computer);
        System.out.println("ma.computer: " + ma.computer.brand);
        System.out.println("-----line 5-----");
        computer = null; //.....................5
        System.out.println("computer: " + computer);
        System.out.println("ma.computer: " + ma.computer);
        ma = new MainApp(); //..................6
        System.out.println("-----line 6-----");
        System.out.println("computer: " + computer);
        System.out.println("ma.computer: " + ma.computer);
    }
}
```

Output

```
-----line 1-----
computer: DELL
-----line 2-----
computer: DELL
ma.computer: null
-----line 3-----
computer: Computer@251a69d7
ma.computer: Computer@251a69d7
-----line 4-----
computer: Computer@7344699f
ma.computer: DELL
-----line 5-----
computer: null
ma.computer: Computer@251a69d7
-----line 6-----
computer: null
ma.computer: null
```

# Answer Exercise 1

## First Option

- The customer class creates an account object when it is unnecessary.
- To prove this point, we added some control to the program.

- We add a no-argument constructor to the class Account with a statement that prints the text "Account is created!" whenever an account object is created as follows.

**Account.java**

```java
public class Account
{
  private String username;
  private String password;

  public Account()
  {
    System.out.println("Account is created!");
  }
}
```

Within the constructor of the class customer, we print the account attribute and the account parameter to know whether the objects are the same.

**Customer.java**

```java
public class Customer
{
  Account account; // remove = new Account();

  public Customer(Account account)
  {
    System.out.println("Account attribute: " + this.account);
    System.out.println("Account argument:  " + account);
    this.account = account;
  }
}
```

In the main method, we create one Customer object to see what happens.

**MainApp.java**

```java
public class MainApp
{
  public static void main(String[] args)
  {
    Account account = new Account();
    Customer customer = new Customer(account);
  }
```

```
}
```

The text within the account constructor is twice printed in the following output, and the two account objects are differen

Output

```
Account is created!
Account attribute: null
Account argument:  Account@7344699f
```

Creating the account object is unnecessary. Therefore, we removed the new Account() statement from the code.

**Customer.java**

```java
public class Customer
{
  Account account; // remove = new Account();

  public Customer(Account account)
  {
    System.out.println("Account attribute: " + this.account);
    System.out.println("Account argument:  " + account);
    this.account = account;
  }
}
```

In a small code like this, creating an object unnecessarily more than you need is not a big issue. Suppose you work with a more extensive application with hundreds of objects and more. That will make a difference.

## Second Option

Another option is to create a no-argument constructor within the class Customer and create the account object within that constructor. We placed some checkpoints to prove that we made only one account object.

**Account.java**

```java
public class Account
```

```java
{
  private String username;
  private String password;

  public Account()
  {
    System.out.println("Account is created!");
  }
}
```

## Customer.java

```java
public class Customer
{
  Account account; // remove = new Account();

  public Customer()
  {
    this.account = new Account();
    System.out.println("Object A: " + account);
  }
  public Customer(Account account)
  {
    System.out.println("Account attribute: " + this.account);
    System.out.println("Account argument:  " + account);
    this.account = account;
  }
}
```

## MainApp.java

```java
public class MainApp
{
  public static void main(String[] args)
  {
    Customer customer = new Customer();
    System.out.println("Object B: " + customer.account);
  }
}
```

The output below shows that only one account object is created.

```
Account is created!
Object A: Account@251a69d7
```

Object B: Account@251a69d7

# 14. Writing clean code

Programs obediently follow a programmer's commands, lacking the ability to determine whether they are written correctly or incorrectly. Once they successfully pass through the compiler's requirements, the code functions. However, mere functionality does not naturally mean professionalism or lack thereof. Professionals commonly evaluate code based on specific criteria.

When writing code, it's crucial to consider that software projects evolve endlessly over time. They often reuse the same logical structures and methods to process input and generate output.
Failure to attach to some particular principles that I explain in this chapter indicates to experts that your code may lack a professional touch. This, in turn, could open the door to issues such as bugs, memory leaks, hacks, maintainability problems, a lack of reusability, and security vulnerabilities.

## Modularization

The process of breaking software into smaller manageable components is known as modularization. The advantage of this process is improving maintainability, reusability, and debugging issues faster and more efficiently. Another advantage of modularization is the ability of a team of programmers to work simultaneously to update the program without conflicts.

## Appropriate Data Types and Names

By choosing the names of objects and attributes, use the camel case. The rule of the camel case is by multiple words; the first word begins in lowercase, but the other words are in uppercase; examples are age, itemValue, and myShoppingCart.

Classes in Java start with uppercase, while methods start with lowercase. Examples of class names are Vehicle, University, and BankAccount. Examples of method names are saveData, printData, setName, and getValue.

If an attribute is a constant, use the final keyword. For example, a week consists of seven days. That shouldn't be accidentally changed. The final keyword prevents unintentionally changing the values of the constant. That applies also to other constants of the application. Suppose a specific attribute is required to be used in the whole application; then consider making it static. Only one copy of a static attribute is available, independent of objects.

## Single Responsibility Principle (SRP)

One of the fundamental principles of designing software is to keep each component taking a single responsibility. If you write a method with multiple responsibilities, reconsider the design and avoid making your code complex.

### *Example 1A: Single Responsibility Principle (SRP)*

The method getCompanyInfo prints the company information such as name, logo, contact, and products.
This method doesn't apply the previously mentioned single responsibility principle SRP.
How can you improve it by applying the rule and printing all the information needed?

**Contact.java**

```java
public class Contact
{
    String street;
    String houseNr;
    String zipCode;
    String city;
    String country;
    String phone;
```

```java
  public Contact()
  {
    this.street = "495 party street";
    this.houseNr = "34A";
    this.zipCode = "NY 10014";
    this.city = "New York";
    this.country = "USA";
    this.phone = "0322-38877290";
  }
}
```

## Company.java

```java
import java.util.ArrayList;

public class Company
{
  private String name;
  private String logo;
  private Contact contact;
  private ArrayList<String> products;

  public Company()
  {
    this.name = "Microsystem";
    this.contact = new Contact();
    this.products = new ArrayList<String>();
    products.add("Software");
    products.add("Database");
  }
  public void getCompanyInfo()
  {
    System.out.println("");
    System.out.println("..........LOGO..........");
    System.out.println("");
    System.out.println(".. Company: " + name + " ..");
    System.out.println("");
    System.out.println(".. Contact Information ..");
    System.out.println("Streer: .......... " + contact.street);
    System.out.println("Appartment: ....... " + contact.houseNr);
    System.out.println("City: ............ " + contact.city);
    System.out.println("Zip code: ........ " + contact.zipCode);
    System.out.println("Country: ......... " + contact.country);
    System.out.println("Phone: ........... " + contact.phone);
    System.out.println("");
    int i = 0;
    System.out.println("");
    System.out.println(".. " + name + " Products ..");
    System.out.println("");

    for (String product : products)
    {
```

```java
      i++;
      System.out.println("Product" + i + ": ......... " + product);
    }
  }
  public static void main(String[] args)
  {
    Company comp = new Company();
    comp.getCompanyInfo();
  }
}
```

**CompanyApp.java**

```java
public class CompanyApp
{
  public static void main(String[] args)
  {
    Company comp = new Company();
    comp.getCompanyInfo();
  }
}
```

Output

```
..........LOGO.........

.. Company: Microsystem ..

.. Contact Information ..
Streer: ........... 495 party street
Appartment: ....... 34A
City: ............. New York
Zip code: ........ NY 10014
Country: .......... USA
Phone: ........... 0322-38877290



.. Microsystem Products ..

Product1: ......... Software
Product2: ......... Database
```

# Explanation

The method getCompanyInfo handles different functions at the same time.
Suppose you need only the company logo or the contact data in the
program, or you want only the company's name and products.

This method is not flexible; it prints everything and is fixed in one order. The question is how we make the method flexible.

You can split the method getCompanyInfo() into four methods that get the logo, the company name, the contact info, and the company's products separately. As shown below, you can invoke those three methods within the method getCompanyInfo(). The rest of the code and the class remains the same.

That will help use only the needed method. And keep the info in the desired order to avoid getting all the information simultaneously.

## Example 1B: Single Responsibility Principle (SRP)

**Company.java**

```java
import java.util.ArrayList;

public class Company
{
  private String name;
  private String logo;
  private Contact contact;
  private ArrayList<String> products;

  public Company()
  {
    this.name = "Microsystem";
    this.contact = new Contact();
    this.products = new ArrayList<String>();
    products.add("Software");
    products.add("Database");
  }
  public void getCompanyLogo()
  {
    System.out.println("");
    System.out.println("...........LOGO..........");
  }
  public void getCompanyName()
  {
    System.out.println("");
    System.out.println(".. Company: " + name + " ..");
  }
  public void getCompanyContact()
  {
    System.out.println("");
    System.out.println("Streer: ........... " + contact.street);
```

```java
      System.out.println("Appartment: ....... " + contact.houseNr);
      System.out.println("City: ............ " + contact.city);
      System.out.println("Zip code: ........ " + contact.zipCode);
      System.out.println("Country: ......... " + contact.country);
      System.out.println("Phone: ........... " + contact.phone);
    }
  public void getCompanyProducts()
  {
    System.out.println("");
    int i = 0;
    System.out.println("");
    System.out.println(".. " + name + " Products ..");
    System.out.println("");

    for (String product : products)
    {
      i++;
      System.out.println("Product" + i + ": ......... " + product);
    }
  }
  public void getCompanyInfo()
  {
    getCompanyLogo();
    getCompanyName();
    getCompanyContact();
    getCompanyProducts();
  }
}
```

By splitting the method getCompany, the split methods can be invoked
individually. You can also use them to work together to display any
information combinations and determine their order.

Output

```
...........LOGO.........

.. Company: Microsystem ..

Streer: .......... 495 party street
Appartment: ....... 34A
City: ............ New York
Zip code: ........ NY 10014
Country: ......... USA
Phone: ........... 0322-38877290


.. Microsystem Products ..
```

```
Product1: .......... Software
Product2: ......... Database
```

## Reusability

The logic repeated in programming is that a piece of code is often needed in many parts and components of the program. Therefore, copying the code in each part where it is required increases the risk of making mistakes and spreading the possible errors in many places in the entire program. That raises the possibility of bugs and makes it hard to find them. Meanwhile, you can write a single logic and reuse it repeatedly. Once you find a bug in the logic or want to update it, you can fix it and update it in fewer places, and it will be set in all the other components that implement it. That will also eliminate the necessity of updating the code and working on it everywhere in the program.

Let's apply the principles explained here and convert them into pieces of code.

### *Example 2A: Reusable Methods*

A car seller requires software to manage the information about his cars, trucks, and other vehicles. Among the requirements, the client wants the data of his vehicles to be displayed precisely in the same style as follows. Therefore, a programmer writes the following code that displays the data as required. The output is shown below if you compile and run the code. Let's take some time and study the code.

What is your idea about the code written below, knowing that the style below is precisely what the client wants?

```
****************************
            Vehicle
****************************
Brand: ............... BMW
Color: ............... Brown
Fuel: ............... Gasoline
```

**Vehicle.java**

```java
public class Vehicle
{
  private String brand;
  private String color;
  private String fuel;

  public Vehicle(String brand, String color, String fuel)
  {
    this.brand = brand;
    this.color = color;
    this.fuel = fuel;
  }
  public void display()
  {
    System.out.println("\n****************************");
    System.out.println("            Vehicle          ");
    System.out.println("****************************");
    System.out.println("Brand: .............. " + brand);
    System.out.println("Color: .............. " + color);
    System.out.println("Fuel: ............... " + fuel);
  }
  public static void main(String[] args)
  {
    Vehicle vh = new Vehicle("BMW", "Brown", "Gasoline");
    vh.display();
  }
}
```

Output

```
****************************
            Vehicle
****************************
Brand: .............. BMW
Color: .............. Brown
Fuel: .............. Gasoline
```

---

## Notice

Copying and pasting code in software is not a good practice.
The above code is not flexible for reusability, and the method cannot be
overridden. Therefore, it lacks reusability and maintainability.

# Explanation

The program requires the programmer to apply the same style to display all the object's data. In the previous example, there is one object, but you must remember that the program grows over time and will contain tens or even hundreds of objects.

This code is implemented poorly for the following reasons.

- By applying the previous display, the programmer needs to manually implement the display style to other objects, which consumes a lot of time.
- Furthermore, the code is only suitable for copying and pasting and changing the name of the attributes, values, and number of dots based on the length of the attributes. The programmer must count each dot to get the object data to look as required.
- Suppose the client requires an update of the style; for example, change all the dots to asterisk or another symbol. For that minor update, a programmer should open all the implementations of the code everywhere to make those simple changes.
- Suppose a programmer makes some mistakes and uses more numbers of dots than the objects require. Over time, the implementation of the style changes.
- Can you override the method if the vehicle, for example, becomes a superclass of other subclass objects that implement that method? I will expand the code later in this chapter by using a subclass to answer this question.
- All the classes in this program have their copy of the display method. By changing any parts of this implementation, programmers should open the entire class and make the changes everywhere manually.

## *Example 2B: Reusable Methods*

The client wants to expand the program and add the data of their cars and trucks. The principle of IS-A is already explained in the inheritance chapter.

By applying the principle of IS-A, the programmer knows that cars inherit from vehicles because a car is a vehicle. So, he applies the inheritance principle to reuse the code as follows.

The car class inherits the attributes of brand, color, and fuel from the class vehicle and keeps its own attribute number of passengers.

The truck class inherits the attributes of brand, color, and fuel from the class vehicle and keeps its own attribute, the loading weight.

The program code and its output is shown below. How can we implement the requirement and make the program reusable for future expansions?

# Exaplanation

To avoid copying and pasting the display method and unnecessarily using the code in all the classes, we created one class responsible for displaying the data in the same standard style. To print the values, we need a value for each attribute.

So, we use an appropriate Java map for this because maps hold keys and values.

We create a list of the variables and constants we need to write the method; as for the attribute values, see the output of the car attributes above.

```java
public void display()
{
  System.out.println("\n****************************");
  System.out.println("             Vehicle             ");
  System.out.println("****************************");
  System.out.println("Brand: ............... " + brand);
  System.out.println("Color: ............... " + color);
  System.out.println("Fuel: ............... " + fuel);
}
```

## Table 1: Constant Values Reusable Methods

| Constants | Value |
|---|---|
| The number of the asterisk above and under the name | 28 |
| | Remember that sometimes, this number |

| | |
|---|---|
| of the class Car. | could be more if a future attribute is longer than Vehicle. |
| The character above and under the title | * Remember that the client might ask to change this char to a different one, which should be as easy as possible. See the complete code. |
| The number of characters before and after the title. | Calculate the title length. Calculate the half of the char's Length. The name of the class Vechicle should be precisely in the middle of the display style. |
| Title side char | The title Vechicle has space characters on both the right and left sides. Therefore, it is not visible, but that could be another char if needed. |
| Number of the chars from the first letter of the attribute till the first letter of the value is | 23 |
| The char between the attributes and the values | It is a dot, but keep the display flexible to change the dots to other chars or signs. |

## Table 2: Variables Reusable Methods

| Variables | Values |
|---|---|
| The attributes and the values, such as Brand BMW, are keys and values and belong together. | We use a Java map for the attributes and the values because maps have a value for each key. |
| The number of the rows | Inserting as many keys and values in a map as necessary is possible. |

Based on the table above, we create the following class, "DataPrinter," and create a method to display data in all the program parts.

**DataPrinter.java**

```java
import java.util.LinkedHashMap;
import java.util.Map;

public class DataPrinter
{
  /*
   *  CH = Char, SD = Side, TL = Title
   *  NR = Number, CL = Column, LN = Length
   */
  final static int NR_TL_CH = 28;
  final static String TL_CH = "*";
  final static String TL_SD_CH = " ";
  final static int CL_LN = 20;
  final static String CH = ".";

  Map<String, String> displayMap;

  public DataPrinter()
  {
    this.displayMap = new LinkedHashMap<String, String>();
  }
  public void addData(String key, String value)
  {
    displayMap.put(key, value);
  }
  public void display(String title)
  {
    int halfTitleLength = (title.length() / 2);
    int halfCoulmnLength = NR_TL_CH / 2;
    int nrSideTitleChars = halfCoulmnLength - halfTitleLength;
    String charsNeeded = TL_CH.repeat(NR_TL_CH);
    String chTLSd = TL_SD_CH.repeat(nrSideTitleChars);
    System.out.println("\n" + charsNeeded);
    System.out.println(chTLSd+" "+title + " "+chTLSd);
    System.out.println(charsNeeded);
  }
  public void display()
  {
    for (Map.Entry<String, String> e : displayMap.entrySet())
    {
      int keyLength = e.getKey().length();
      int nrChBeKey = CL_LN - keyLength; // nr chars next to key
      String chBeKey = CH.repeat(nrChBeKey); // chars next to key
      System.out.println(e.getKey()+": "+chBeKey+" "+e.getValue());
    }
  }
}
```

By using the class DataPrinter, we can have more control over the most display updates for the whole application.

We implement this method for both Vehicles and Cars.

### Vehicle.java

```java
public class Vehicle
{
  protected String brand;
  protected String color;
  protected String fuel;
  protected DataPrinter dP;

  public Vehicle(String brand, String color, String fuel)
  {
    this.brand = brand;
    this.color = color;
    this.fuel = fuel;
    this.dP = new DataPrinter();
    this.dP.addData("Brand", brand);
    this.dP.addData("Color", color);
    this.dP.addData("Fuel", fuel);
    //System.out.println("VH brand: " +this.brand);
  }
  public void display()
  {
    dP.display();
  }
}
```

### Car.java

```java
public class Car extends Vehicle
{
  private int maxP; // max number passengers
  public Car(String brand, String color, String fuel, int maxP)
  {
    super(brand, color, fuel);
    this.maxP = maxP;
    super.dP.addData("Nr Passengers", String.valueOf(maxP));
  }
  public void display()
  {
    dP.display("CAR");
    dP.display();
  }
}
```

### Truck.java

```java
public class Truck extends Vehicle
{
  private int maxLoad; // in kg

  public Truck(String brand, String color, String fuel, int
maxLoad)
  {
    super(brand, color, fuel);
    this.maxLoad = maxLoad;
    super.dP.addData("Max load in kg", String.valueOf(maxLoad));
  }
  public void display()
  {
    dP.display("TRUCK");
    dP.display();
  }
}
```

### MainApp.java

```java
public class MainApp
{
  public static void main(String[] args)
  {
    Car car = new Car("BMW", "Brown", "Gasoline", 5);
    Truck truck = new Truck("Volvo", "Green", "Gasoline", 12000);

    car.display();
    truck.display();
  }
}
```

### Output

```
***************************
            CAR
***************************
Brand: ............... BMW
Color: ............... Brown
Fuel: ............... Gasoline
Nr Passengers: ....... 5


***************************
           TRUCK
***************************
Brand: ............... Volvo
Color: ............... Green
```

```
Fuel: ................ Gasoline
Max load in kg: ...... 12000
```

# Example 2B Task

What are the answers to the following question? If you make the following
code changes, compile and rerun the program. Look at all the code
implementations in your program.

1. What happens if you change the value of the attribute NR_TL_CH
   from 28 to 30?
2. What happens if you change the asterisk "*" sign of the TL_CH
   attribute to an equal sign '='?
3. What happens if you change the value of TL_SD_CH from space "to
   '.' sign?
4.  1. If you change the value of the attribute CL_LN from 20 to 30, the
   data display changes as follows.
5.  2. If you change the CH attribute value from dot '.' to space," the
   display data is changed as follows.

The previous example shows that programmers would have more control
over their code by creating a template and applying it overall in the
application. Besides, in the long term, a goal could be achieved by writing
much less code, reusing it, and using it in other parts of the program.

The expected output after changin the values of the variables.

```
==================================
............... CAR ..............
==================================
Brand: ......................... BMW
Color: ......................... Brown
Fuel: .......................... Gasoline
Nr Passengers: ................. 5


==================================
.............. TRUCK ............
==================================
Brand: ..................... Volvo
```

```
Color: ...................... Green
Fuel: ....................... Gasoline
Max load in kg: ............. 12000
```

## Exercise 1: Adding Engine Code

Add the "engine code" attribute to the previous Vehicle class, with minimum super and subclass updates. The expected output of the program by adding engine code is shown below.

Output

```
****************************
            CAR
****************************
Brand: ............... BMW
Color: ............... Brown
Fuel: ............... Gasoline
Engine code: ......... ECAR3445
Nr Passengers: ....... 5


****************************
           TRUCK
****************************
Brand: ............... Volvo
Color: ............... Green
Fuel: ................ Gasoline
Engine code: ......... ETRU988
Max load in kg: ...... 12000
```

## Avoid Magic Number

A magic number is a number that is used directly in the code without any explanation of where that number comes from.

Usually, it hides under many lines of code, and it takes a lot of time to find that kind of number by searching it. Suppose you search for it to update it. It isn't easy to locate where it is in the code. An example is using the number within the code that indicates how many times a user can attempt to log in or how many times he can try to guess a secret number.

# *Example 3: Magic Numbers*

The following program generates a secret number and allows the user to guess the number. The code has a magic number indicating the maximum number of attempts the user can guess the number. Can you find that number in the code?

**RandomElement.java**

```java
import java.util.Random;

public class RandomElement
{
  int[] arraySecret = { 1, 2, 3, 4, 5, 6, 7, 8, 9, 10 };

  static int[] intArray = { 1, 2 };

  public static int getRandom(int[] array)
  {
    int rnd = new Random().nextInt(array.length);
    return array[rnd];
  }
}
```

**Secret.java**

```java
import java.util.Scanner;

public class Secret
{
  public static void main(String[] args)
  {
    int rsn = 0; // rsn = random secret number
    int gsn = 0; // gsn = guess number
    int[] arraySecret = { 1, 2, 3, 4, 5, 6, 7, 8, 9, 10 };

    rsn = RandomElement.getRandom(arraySecret);
    System.out.println("\nRandom secret number: " + rsn);
    Scanner input = new Scanner(System.in);
    System.out.print("\nEnter a guess number from 1 to 10: ");
    int i = 0;

    // Check if next input is int
    while (input.hasNextInt())
    {
      i++;
      gsn = input.nextInt();
```

```java
      if(gsn == rsn)
      {
        System.out.println("Guess  " + gsn + " is correct.");
        break;
      }

      if(i >= 3)
      {
        System.out.println("Max is reached secret was: " + rsn);
        break;
      }
      System.out.print("Incorrect, please try again: ");
    }
    System.out.print("Application is closed");
    input.close();
  }
}
```

Output

```
Enter a guess number from 1 to 10: 3
Incorrect, please try again: 4
Incorrect, please try again: 6
Max attempts secret nr: 9
Application is closed
```

## *Exercise 2: Magic Number*

Improve the program and clarify how often the user can guess the number.
Besides, make the code more flexible by allowing the change of that number
to be more accessible.

RandomElement selects a random number from an array used in the class
Secret.

## Hard Coding

"Hard Coding" results in coding that can hide within other parts of the
program, consume time to find and update it, and it is not easy to directly
edit it for new requirements of the software for different reasons; for
example, you have to search the piece of code within the entire or part of the
program to update it.

# Example 4: Hard Coding

The following code prints a menu so the user can select and access the
desired feature.
This code writes all the texts of the menu within the source code. If you
need the menu somewhere else in the program, copy exactly what you see
here. Suppose that other programmers continue with this code and change
the texts and other parts of the menu; then, the menu will be different within
the program.

**Menu.java**

```java
public class Menu
{
  public void printMenu(String accessType)
  {
    System.out.print("\n\n Menu "+"\n .. Insert a letter .. \n");
    System.out.print(" D " + "Display |");
    System.out.print(" S " + "Save  |");
    System.out.print(" X" + " Exit  |");

    if(accessType == "admin")
    {
      System.out.print(" A " + "Add |");
      System.out.print(" R " + "Remove |");
    }
    else if(accessType == "editor")
    {
      System.out.print(" U " + "Update |");
    }
  }
  public static void main(String[] args)
  {
    Menu menu = new Menu();
    menu.printMenu("admin");
    menu.printMenu("editor");
    menu.printMenu("basic");
  }
}
```

The first menu is shown if the user access is admin, the second one is shown
if the user access is editor, but the third one is for users with basic access.

Output

```
Menu
 .. Insert a letter ..
D Display | S Save | X Exit | A Add | R Remove |

Menu
 .. Insert a letter ..
D Display | S Save | X Exit | U Update |

Menu
 .. Insert a letter ..
D Display | S Save | X Exit |
```

## *Exercise 3: Hard Coding Menu*

Improve the previous code and create an enum, for example, to use as a remote control for the whole menu.

## Thinking in Terms of the Future

In software development, clients often need a wide understanding of coding complications but possess a clear vision of the data they require. For instance, a client may initially request only the customer's name or the product's brand. As a programmer, it is crucial to predict future needs. While implementing a solution for the current requirement, such as capturing only a customer's name or a product's brand, it's essential to think ahead.

## *Example 5: Forward Thinking a Bookshop*

Consider the following example in a bookshop's code: the Book class currently defines the book's author as a string. This approach may need to be modified, as it foresees only a singular piece of information about the author. It would be more careful to design the system, predicting that the client may soon require additional details about authors, such as their other works, the genres they specialize in, and other relevant information. By adopting a more comprehensive and forward-thinking approach to coding, we ensure the adaptability of the software to meet growing client needs.

**Book.java**

```java
public class Book
{
  String title;
  String author;

  Book(String title, String author)
  {
    this.title = title;
    this.author = author;
  }
}
```

**MainApp.java**

```java
public class MainApp
{
  public static void main(String[] args)
  {
    Book book = new Book("Subconcious mind", "George Smith");
    System.out.println();
  }
}
```

## *Exercise 4: Bookshop*

Enhance the existing program code to enable the incorporation of additional information about authors in the future. Instead of merely storing the author as a string, consider restructuring the code to adapt a more powerful and extensible representation of author details. For instance, you could create an Author class that encapsulates various attributes related to authors, such as their names, biographies, and ages.

# Answers to the Quizzes and the Exercises

# Answer Exercise 1

In the following code we added the engince code to the program.

**Vehicle.java**

```java
public class Vehicle
{
```

```java
  protected String brand;
  protected String color;
  protected String fuel;
  protected String eCode; // engine code
  protected DataPrinter dP;

  public Vehicle(String brand, String color, String fuel, String
                                                     eCode)
  {
    this.brand = brand;
    this.color = color;
    this.fuel = fuel;
    this.dP = new DataPrinter();
    this.dP.addData("Brand", brand);
    this.dP.addData("Color", color);
    this.dP.addData("Fuel", fuel);
    this.dP.addData("Engine code", eCode);
    //System.out.println("VH brand: " +this.brand);
  }
  public void display()
  {
    dP.display();
  }
}
```

## Car.java

```java
public class Car extends Vehicle
{
  private int maxP; // max number passengers
  public Car(String brand, String color, String fuel, String eCode,
int maxP)
  {
    super(brand, color, fuel, eCode);
    this.maxP = maxP;
    super.dP.addData("Nr Passengers", String.valueOf(maxP));
  }
  public void display()
  {
    dP.display("CAR");
    dP.display();
  }
}
```

## Truck.java

```java
public class Truck extends Vehicle
{
  private int maxLoad; // in kg

  public Truck(String brand, String color, String fuel, String
```

```java
                                        engineCode, int maxLoad)
  {
    super(brand, color, fuel, engineCode);
    this.maxLoad = maxLoad;
    super.dP.addData("Max load in kg", String.valueOf(maxLoad));
  }
  public void display()
  {

    dP.display("TRUCK");
    dP.display();
  }
}
```

## DataPrinter.java

```java
import java.util.LinkedHashMap;
import java.util.Map;

public class DataPrinter
{
  /*
   *  CH = Char, SD = Side, TL = Title
   *  NR = Number, CL = Column, LN = Length
   */
  final static int NR_TL_CH = 28;
  final static String TL_CH = "*";
  final static String TL_SD_CH = " ";
  final static int CL_LN = 20;
  final static String CH = ".";

  Map<String, String> displayMap;

  public DataPrinter()
  {
    this.displayMap = new LinkedHashMap<String, String>();
  }
  public void addData(String key, String value)
  {
    displayMap.put(key, value);
  }
  public void display(String title)
  {
    int halfTitleLength = (title.length() / 2);
    int halfCoulmnLength = NR_TL_CH / 2;
    int nrSideTitleChars = halfCoulmnLength - halfTitleLength;
    String charsNeeded = TL_CH.repeat(NR_TL_CH);
    String chTLSd = TL_SD_CH.repeat(nrSideTitleChars);
    System.out.println("\n" + charsNeeded);
    System.out.println(chTLSd+" "+title + " "+chTLSd);
    System.out.println(charsNeeded);
  }
  public void display()
```

```java
  {
    for (Map.Entry<String, String> e : displayMap.entrySet())
    {
      int keyLength = e.getKey().length();
      int nrChBeKey = CL_LN - keyLength; // nr chars next to key
      String chBeKey = CH.repeat(nrChBeKey); // chars next to key
      System.out.println(e.getKey()+": "+chBeKey+" "+e.getValue());
    }
  }
}
```

## MainApp.java

```java
public class MainApp
{
  public static void main(String[] args)
  {
    Vehicle vh = new Vehicle("Cadilac", "Red", "Gasoline",
"EC59494");
    Car car = new Car("BMW", "Brown", "Gasoline", "ECAR3445", 5);
    Truck truck = new Truck("Volvo", "Green", "Gasoline",
"ETRU988", 12000);
    car.display();
    truck.display();
  }
}
```

# Answer Exercise 2

The number 3 that is used is actually the maximum attempts that the user may guess the secret number. By declaring a variable above the code and calling it maxAttempts makes the code clear and you can easily change the maximum number as often as you want.

## RandomElement.java

```java
import java.util.Random;

public class RandomElement
{
  int[] arraySecret = { 1, 2, 3, 4, 5, 6, 7, 8, 9, 10 };

  static int[] intArray = { 1, 2 };

  public static int getRandom(int[] array)
  {
    int rnd = new Random().nextInt(array.length);
    return array[rnd];
  }
```

```
}
```

## Secret.java

```java
import java.util.Scanner;

public class Secret
{
  public static void main(String[] args)
  {
    int rsn = 0; // rsn = random secret number
    int gsn = 0; // gsn = guess number
    int maxAttempts = 3; // maximum attempts
    int[] arraySecret = { 1, 2, 3, 4, 5, 6, 7, 8, 9, 10 };

    rsn = RandomElement.getRandom(arraySecret);
    // uncomment the following line to display the secret number
    // System.out.println("\nRandom secret number: " + rsn);
    Scanner input = new Scanner(System.in);
    System.out.print("\nEnter a guess number from 1 to 10: ");
    int i = 0;

    // Check if next input is int
    while (input.hasNextInt())
    {
      i++;
      gsn = input.nextInt();

      if(gsn == rsn)
      {
        System.out.println("Guess  " + gsn + " is correct.");
        break;
      }

      if(i >= maxAttempts) // replace number 3 with maxAttempts
      {
        System.out.println("Max is reached secret was: " + rsn);
        break;
      }
      System.out.print("Incorrect, please try again: ");
    }
    System.out.print("Application is closed");
    input.close();
  }
}
```

# Answer Exercise 3

In Java, enum is used for constants. In this case, consider using an enum for all the texts and the menus to change the menu and the access there.

**Menu.java**

```java
public class Menu
{
  public void printMenu(AccessTE accessTE)
  {
    System.out.print(MenuIE.SELECT.getCode() +
                                MenuIE.SELECT.getName());
    System.out.print(MenuIE.DISPLAY.getCode() +
                                MenuIE.DISPLAY.getName());
    System.out.print(MenuIE.SAVE.getCode() +
                                MenuIE.SAVE.getName());
    System.out.print(MenuIE.EXIT.getCode() +
                                MenuIE.EXIT.getName());

    if(accessTE == AccessTE.ADMIN)
    {
      System.out.print(MenuIE.ADD.getCode() +
                                MenuIE.ADD.getName());
      System.out.print(MenuIE.REMOVE.getCode() +
                                MenuIE.REMOVE.getName());
    }
    else if(accessTE == AccessTE.EDITOR)
    {
      System.out.print(MenuIE.UPDATE.getCode() +
                                MenuIE.UPDATE.getName());
    }
  }
  public static void main(String[] args)
  {
    Menu menu = new Menu();
    menu.printMenu(AccessTE.ADMIN);
    menu.printMenu(AccessTE.EDITOR);
    menu.printMenu(AccessTE.BASIC);
  }
}
```

**Enum: AccessTE.java**

```java
// AccessType Enum = AccessTE
public enum AccessTE
{
  ADMIN, EDITOR, BASIC;
}
```

### Enum: MenuIE

```java
// MenuItemEnum = MenuIE
public enum MenuIE
{
  ACCESS_TYPE("ADMIN", "Adiministrator"),
  SELECT("\n\n Menu ", "\n ... Insert a letter ... \n"),
  ACCESS("\n\n Menu ", "\n ... You cannot access the
                                      application ... \n"),
  ADD(" A ", "Add |"), // access admin
  DISPLAY(" D ", "Display |"), // access admin, editor and basic
  SAVE(" S ", "Save |"), // access admin, editor
  REMOVE(" R ", "Remove |"), // access admin, editor
  UPDATE(" U ", "Update |"), // access admin, editor
  EXIT(" X", " Exit |"); // // access admin, editor and basic
  private String code;
  private String name;

  MenuIE(String code, String name)
  {
    this.code = code;
    this.name = name;
  }
  public String getCode()
  {
    return code;
  }
  public String getName()
  {
    return name;
  }
}
```

# Answer Exercise 4

### Author.java

```java
public class Author
{
  String name;
  String biography;
  int age;

  public Author(String name, int age)
  {
    this.name = name;
    this.age = age;
  }
```

```
}
```

## Book.java

```java
public class Book
{
  String title;
  Author author;

  Book(String title, Author author)
  {
    this.title = title;
    this.author = author;
  }
}
```

## MainApp.java

```java
public class MainApp
{
  public static void main(String[] args)
  {
    Author author = new Author("George", 43);
    Book book = new Book("Subconcious mind", author);
    System.out.println("Title: " + book.title);
    System.out.println("Author name: " + author.name);
    System.out.println("Author age: " + author.age);
  }
}
```

Output

```
Title: Subconcious mind
Author name: George
Author age: 43
```

# Alphabetical Index

# W